THE FANTASY FOOTBALL BLACK BOOK
2024 Edition

By: Joe Pisapia
@JoePisapia17

Featuring

Andrew Erickson @AndrewErickson
Derek Brown @DBro_FFB
Scott Bogman @BogmanSports
Evan Tarracciano @Roto_Wizard
Edited by Mike Maher @mikeMaher

Cover Art by Ethan Woodward
Graphics by EJ Vitez

©2024 Joe Pisapia, LLC
Fantasy Black Book Sports, All Rights Reserved
Facebook: Fantasy Black Book

RPV CHEAT SHEETS NOW AVAILABLE!

Want all the RPV for every format on one easy-to-reference cheat sheet PDF file?
Plus, <u>FREE</u> updates sent in July & Aug!?

Send $5 to:
PayPal: fantasyblackbook@gmail.com
or
Venmo: @FantasyBlackBook
Be sure to write:
"Cheat Sheets" & add your <u>email address</u> in the comments!

About the Authors:

Joe Pisapia (@JoePisapia17 Twitter/IG, @fantasyprojoe TikTok)
Joe is the author of the #1 best-selling Fantasy Black Book Series on Amazon and creator of the revolutionary player evaluation tool Relative Position Value (RPV). He's the host of the FantasyPros Fantasy Football Podcast, FantasyProsMLB Leading Off Podcast, and BettingPros Podcast. Joe is also currently the host of "Fantasy Sports Today on SportsGridTV.

Derek Brown *is a senior fantasy football analyst at FantasyPros. He's written previously for FTN, Playerprofiler, & FantasyData. Derek is a perennial contributor to the Fantasy Football Black Book. His DFS, redraft, and dynasty takes have been previously projected to the masses with recurring guest roles on Sirius XM and DK Sweat. Born in Louisiana, he is a diehard Saints fan (Whodat).*

Andrew Erickson *has been in the fantasy football space since 2017, but he finally got his break in the full-time business with PFF in 2020. He's since taken his talents to nerds over FantasyPros joining forced with Joe Pisapia and Derek Brown. He rests his laurels on living life by the 6 Fs: Family, Friends, Food, Fitness and Fantasy Football.*

Scott Bogman *has been in the Fantasy Sports industry since 2014, co-hosting Fantasy Football, Fantasy College Football and Fantasy Baseball shows for In This League as well as hosting the FantasyPros Dynasty Fantasy Football Podcast. Bogman also contributes to SportsGrid and CFB Winning Edge. This will be his 4th year contributing rookie profiles and 3rd covering IDPs for the Black Book. You can find his work by following him on Twitter @BogmanSports or check out the In This League Patreon at Patreon.com/ITLArmy!*

Evan Tarracciano *FantasyPros featured writer and content creator. Fantasy Football Personality, Award-winning author and Sirius XM guest contributor.*

Mike Maher *is the Senior Manager, Content at FantasyPros & BettingPros. In a previous life, he worked in book publishing for more than a decade, including several years as the Digital Operations Manager at one of the largest book publishers in the world, HarperCollins Publishers. But the allure of FantasyPros was too strong, and he made the jump from long-time freelancer to full-timer in March of 2022. He is also currently pursuing a Master of Professional Studies degree at George Washington University. When not talking about fantasy sports, sports betting, books, Chaim Bloom, AI, or the Eagles, he works on being a good dad to Nolan and Juliet, a good husband to Courtney, and adapting to life in Georgia.*

TABLE OF CONTENTS

Chapter 1 The "E.C.O." System: Expected Cumulative Offense

Chapter 2 RPV: Relative Position Value

Chapter 3 Draft Strategies 2024

Chapter 4 Quarterback Profiles

Chapter 5 Running Back Profiles

Chapter 6 Wide Receive Profiles

Chapter 7 Tight End Profiles

Chapter 8 D/ST Profiles

Chapter 9 IDP (Individual Defensive Players)

Chapter 10 Kickers

Chapter 11 Dynasty Strategy

Chapter 12 NFL Team Previews 2024

Chapter 1

The "E.C.O." System
Expected Cumulative Offense System

Joe Pisapia

To continue my goal of making fantasy football strategy more effective and applicable, I wanted to find a way to quantify how we should be investing in players. For quite some time, I've been discussing offensive ecosystems and why talent isn't enough for players to be productive. Environment is equally key for great talents to become great fantasy talents. But, how do we quantify what's a good environment? I'm glad you asked. What I've done this year is take every NFL offense and grade their Head Coach, Quarterback, Offensive Line and Skill Players on a simple 1-5 scale. Then take an average for each team to determine which teams we should be targeting with our fantasy draft capital.

Now, it seems simplistic to say, "draft good players on good teams", but often we realize we get intoxicated by a dynamic rookie in a rocky situation or an established veteran who's been fantasy-relevant for years moving to a lesser team, and we expect the production to carry over only to be let down. The "E.C.O." System (or Expected Cumulative Offense), takes some of that guesswork out and splashes some cold water on the overhyped. There will always be outliers to even a strong concept, and I even went so far as to identify who I think can overachieve and fly up the ranks of the "E.C.O" System and outperform their ranking. However, the intent here is to fix our concentration in our fantasy investments in the offenses that are positioned to succeed and fade those that may have some intrigue but are set up for failure.

The Elite

TEAM	QB	HC	OL	SKILL	OVERALL	LEVEL
	5	5	5	4	★★★★★	ELITE
	5	4	5	5	★★★★★	ELITE
	4	5	4	5	★★★★★	ELITE
	5	5	4	3	★★★★★	ELITE
	5	3	4	5	★★★★★	ELITE
	4	4	5	4	★★★★★	ELITE
	3	4	5	5	★★★★★	ELITE
	3	5	4	5	★★★★★	ELITE

These teams are the cream of the fantasy crop. Constructing fantasy rosters with a concentration of these players should yield very positive results as long as the QB element stays healthy. When an elite QB goes down, all bets are off on the other skill players succeeding. Now, this doesn't just mean the obvious Ja'Marr Chases of the world, but also later round picks like the Zack Moss or even the Jermaine Burton types as well. When you get into later rounds, players like Burton could benefit from injuries ahead of them on the depth chart, resulting in them stepping into lead roles in strong situations. Take Zack Moss last year with the Colts. Jonathan Taylor held out and had injuries and Zack Moss stepped in and was wildly productive. Most didn't see this coming, but the Colts "E.C.O." system had strong HC and OL scores, helping the cause. The Colts continue to be the sexy team on this list this season. The rest of this group is the usual suspects, but the Rams are a sneaky team to invest in for 2024.

The Strong

Team	QB	HC	OL	SKILL	STARS	LEVEL
	4	3	4	5	★★★★	STRONG
	5	4	3	4	★★★★	STRONG
	4	2	5	5	★★★★	STRONG

These three teams have strong investment potential, but each has some questions to account for, starting with the Texans. Houston was the Cinderella story of last season, and they added Stefon Diggs and Joe Mixon. However, the offensive line had a ton of injuries last year, and now they're no longer a team playing the underdog, but playing the favorite. We don't know how they will react to that pressure. The Cowboys got elite fantasy seasons from Dak Prescott and CeeDee Lamb, but the rest was mid at best, and their run game and coaching remain suspect. Then there are the Falcons. I'm very excited about the possibilities when I think of Kirk Cousins with all that young talent. But, realistically, it's a new system, new city, new staff… lots of new things can take a while to come together. I would still invest in these three environments, but with my eyes wide open.

Above Average

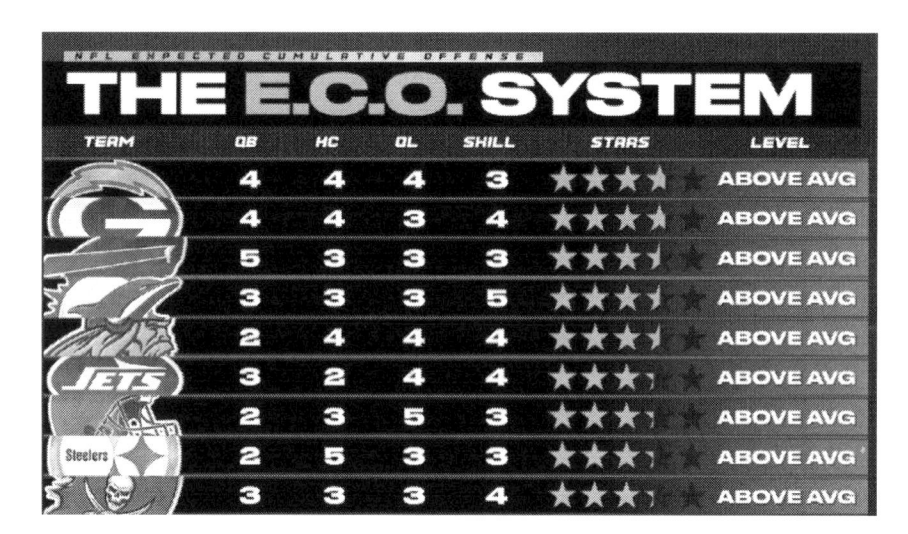

Team	QB	HC	OL	SKILL	STARS	LEVEL
	4	4	4	3	★★★★	ABOVE AVG
	4	4	3	4	★★★★	ABOVE AVG
	5	3	3	3	★★★	ABOVE AVG
	3	3	3	5	★★★	ABOVE AVG
	2	4	4	4	★★★	ABOVE AVG
Jets	3	2	4	4	★★★	ABOVE AVG
	2	3	5	3	★★★	ABOVE AVG
Steelers	2	5	3	3	★★★	ABOVE AVG
	3	3	3	4	★★★	ABOVE AVG

This next group is where you can build your depth and volume. Some teams, like the Chargers, are coming off down seasons but have the right pieces to bounce back. Some were pleasant surprises, like the Packers and Buccaneers, while others could take a step backward like the Buffalo Bills. The Chargers, Packers, Dolphins and Bucs would be where I would invest within this grouping for the best combination of floor and upside. The others have far more downside scenarios.

Below Average and The Overachiever

THE E.C.O. SYSTEM
NFL EXPECTED CUMULATIVE OFFENSE

TEAM	QB	HC	OL	SKILL	OVERALL	LEVEL
	3	3	2	4	★★★	AVERAGE
	3	2	3	4	★★★	AVERAGE
	3	3	2	3	★★★	BELOW AVERAGE
	4	2	1	3	★★	OUTLIER
	1	2	3	4	★★	BELOW AVERAGE
	1	3	3	3	★★	BELOW AVERAGE
	2	1	2	4	★★	BELOW AVERAGE

This group has some serious "buzz" with the new-look Chicago Bears and the very exciting Jayden Daniels now in Washington. However, this group isn't a lock to be great, or even average. The one team I would identify as a potential outlier candidate is the Cardinals. They have a healthy Kyler Murray, a stud TE in Trey McBride, and drafted one of the best wide receiver prospects in recent years in Marvin Harrsion Jr. What holds them back potentially is that offensive line and lingering concerns about Jonathan Gannon's coaching ability. Those negatives aside, the new running back depth is also encouraging there, and I believe the Cardinals are best poised to jump from "Below" to "Above" average status.

Avoid

THE E.C.O. SYSTEM
NFL EXPECTED CUMULATIVE OFFENSE

TEAM	QB	HC	OL	SKILL	STARS	LEVEL
	2	3	1	2	★★	AVOID
	2	1	2	3	★★	AVOID
	1	2	2	2	★★	AVOID
	2	1	1	2	★	AVOID
	1	1	2	1	★	AVOID

Investing in these situations can potentially burn your fantasy season to the ground. Too many questions, too many concerns. Sure, weird things happen in football, but even as you get later into drafts, I would rather be committing to guys a little further down the depth charts on great offenses, instead of higher depth chart players in dire situations. Alvin Kamara and Chris Olave stand out as individual outliers with veteran Derek Carr, but it could be dicey as Carr continues to decline. Fantasy productivity can certainly come from bad NFL teams. But it rarely comes from situations with bad QB/O-Line/HC situations.

So, there you have it. A snapshot of fantasy "investability". Use it wisely!

Chapter 2

RPV: Relative Position Value

Joe Pisapia

"The format and style of your league dictates the value of a player more than the talent of that player."

Rankings are good. Tiered Rankings are better. QUANTIFIED Rankings specific to your scoring system are best!

This is the creed of The Fantasy Black Book over the years and why **Relative Position Value (RPV)** is a difference maker for so many fantasy players over the last decade. If it didn't work, we wouldn't sell this many books and cheat sheets every season. There are other value systems out there, but they fall woefully short because they either look at positions as a whole or work solely on projections. RPV works of a hybrid of projections, previous season stats and three-year averages when applicable. With rookies, college stats get factored into projections along with previous seasons stats of the role they're assuming with their new NFL offense to make sure the picture is as clear as possible for their outlook. However, the biggest key to why RPV is superior is the fact it understands RB isn't a position, but RB1 is. Most teams in your league will have an RB1, a WR1, WR2 etc. So, how do you draft to create core roster strength and create an edge over your opponents? By using the RPV system to evaluate talent and build your roster. RPV goes beyond well-informed analysis and creates a tangible strategy. When you combine both, as we do in the Black Book, you will be unstoppable.

Chances are you're playing in multiple leagues, with a myriad of different rules and scoring. That's why I created Relative Position Value (RPV), the one tool to rule them all. Even if you play in the oddest scoring on the planet, you can use the formula yourself and get a basic working model of how to approach your draft and evaluate in season trades using RPV. The RPV key will unlock your ability to maximize the available active roster spots you have on your team on a weekly basis.

RPV will automatically create player tiers -- and *define* them. It will also tell you how strong or weak a position player pool is entering the season. RPV is completely adaptable and adjustable to all league styles, depths and scoring systems. It's the single most useful player evaluation system available to fantasy owners and perhaps one of the easiest to grasp. I like simple and effective. RPV is both.

So, remember when I said, "RB isn't a position, but RB1 is"? Well, let's dive into that and explain in more detail how RPV works and how to apply it.

STRIKING A BALANCE

It doesn't matter that Player A is ranked two slots above Player B on some "experts' board." What REALLY matters is how much more productive Player A is than Player B -- and how much better they are than the other options at their position. Projections can be helpful, but not relied upon solely. When's the last time projectionists were held accountable (or held themselves accountable) for their many failures? The answer is hardly ever. Projections can have their place when you couple them with reality.

RPV compiles projections, previous season stats and three-year averages (when applicable) before weighing them to create a Black Book Point Total. That number is ALWAYS format-specific and is historically more reliable than projections alone, hence the success of the Black Book series. When it comes to rookies or young players, clearly, we must rely more heavily on projections but use a cross-section to do so.

Now, what happens next to that Black Book Point Totals?

RPV IN THEORY

"RB isn't a position, BUT RB1 is!"

Considering a base of a 12-team league with two active RBs each week, a group of 24 running backs is a good starting point to grasp the RPV concept. However, it's NOT how we're going to truly utilize the tool.

Over 16 games in 2023, Christian McCaffrey led all PPR running backs with 391 pts in PPR scoring. Rachaad White ranked fourth with 269 pts. The 12th-best running back was James Cook at 232, and the 24th was De'Von Achane with 190.

So, how much more valuable is each one of these guys compared to the other? Before we get ahead of ourselves, let's first see the formula in action.

The Fantasy Black Book formula is more complicated than the "basic" version I will present to you here. At the core, the way to determine the RPV -- or the percentage in which a player is better than the fantasy league average -- is:

(Individual Player Point Value – Fantasy League Average of the Position) ÷ Fantasy League Average of the Position = RPV

So, what is "Fantasy League Average?" Well, every league has a different number of teams and a varying number of active players at a given position. Some have 1RB/3WR/1FLEX, others play 2QB/2RB/3WR, and the list goes on and on.

The Fantasy League Average is a position's average production, based on the depth of your league. For example, if your league has 12 managers and starts two running backs every week, the RB pool is 24 total. If the top player scored 250 points and the 24th scored around 120, the fantasy league's scoring average is likely somewhere around 185 points. All players who score above this mark are "Positive RPV" players. The ones below are "Negative RPV."

Fantasy sports is a simple game of outscoring your opponents as frequently as possible from as many active positions as you can. The more your team lives in the "Positive," the greater your chances are week-to-week. It's like playing the odds in Texas hold'em. If you have a strong starting hand, the odds are in your favor. Sure, you may take some "bad beats", but often, the percentages will play in your favor.

Here's the trick! Even though there are 24 running backs, almost every team will likely have **one true RB1**, which means RB1 is its own unique scoring position. Rather than create a Fantasy League Average for 24 overall backs, it's more applicable to separate RB1s and RB2s into their own private groups and create an individual fantasy league average for each.

Now that we understand Fantasy League Average, let's get more specific. Last year, Christian McCaffrey scored **391** (full point PPR) pts. The Fantasy League Average (or FLA) at RB1 last year (top 12) in PPR scoring was **268** pts.

Subtract that FLA (268 pts) from McCaffrey's 391 pts, then divide by that same FLA (268 pts) using the simple formula:

Relative Position Value of +46% RPV: [391-269] ÷ 268 = 46%.

Christina McCaffrey was a +46% RPV better than the Fantasy League Average RB1 in 2023. #Quantified!!!

That means CMC was 46% more productive than the average RB1 in fantasy leagues in PPR scoring.

That's substantial! That's not theoretical, it's definitive. That means something!

If we took the RPV of running back as a whole over the top 24, CMC's RPV would jump to a whopping +65% RPV, because the Fantasy League Average would be just 236 pts, creating a larger divide.

BUT we don't do that, because he'll be stacking up, head-to-head, against other RB1s most weeks in theoretical terms against other RB1 slots on other rosters. Calculating RB1s and RB2s as their individual positions gives a much more accurate depiction of a player's value, hence what makes RPV better than other value-based systems.

Are you in a 14-team league? Then use the top 14 to establish RB1 RPV. In a 10- team league? Adjust that way. The deeper the league, the more difficult it is to create an RPV advantage. The shallower the league, the less disparity you'll find (especially at WR). Therefore, you have more options to construct your roster in different ways. Have a wacky scoring system? Doesn't matter. RPV formula covers everything.

Below is the **Final RPV** for RB1s and RB2s from the end of 2023. You'll see not only the positive but also the negative side of RPV. The avoidance of over drafting/overspending on players that can't really supply you with "positive" production or as I like to say, 'move the needle". This clears the path to success. You will also see as we go on how to create an RPV advantage.

2023 FINAL RB RPV for RB1 and RB2 (Full PPR scoring)

	RB 1 PPR	FPTS	RPV
1	Christian McCaffrey (SF)	391.3	46%
2	Breece Hall (NYJ)	290.5	8%
3	Travis Etienne Jr. (JAC)	282.4	5%
4	Rachaad White (TB)	267.9	0%
5	Raheem Mostert (MIA)	267.7	0%
6	Joe Mixon (CIN)	267	-1%
7	Kyren Williams (LAR)	255	-5%
8	Derrick Henry (TEN)	246.7	-8%
9	Bijan Robinson (ATL)	246.3	-8%
10	Jahmyr Gibbs (DET)	242.1	-10%
11	Alvin Kamara (NO)	233	-13%
12	James Cook (BUF)	232.7	-13%

	RB2 PPR	FPTS	RPV
13	Saquon Barkley (NYG)	223.2	9%
14	Tony Pollard (DAL)	222.6	9%
15	Isiah Pacheco (KC)	213.9	4%
16	Jerome Ford (CLE)	211.2	3%
17	David Montgomery (DET)	207.2	1%
18	James Conner (ARI)	201.5	-2%
19	Kenneth Walker III (SEA)	199.4	-3%
20	D'Andre Swift (PHI)	199.3	-3%
21	Brian Robinson Jr. (WAS)	198.1	-3%
22	Jaylen Warren (PIT)	196.4	-4%
23	Najee Harris (PIT)	195.5	-5%
24	De'Von Achane (MIA)	190.7	-7%

You can see from last year's RPV not only the distinct advantage. It was CMC and then basically the field. Kyren Williams came on strong at the end, as did Jahmyr Gibbs. Saquon Barkley and Tony Pollard were drafted as #1 RBs, but both finished as RB2's and that hurt you based upon their draft day price. The good news is that only one team will have the "difference maker" that is McCaffrey. Therefore, the remaining running back board is made of a few clumps in 2024. The three down backs, the specialists (PPR guys or standard league TD guys) and then the rookies who may come on strong in the second half. There will be "safe" options like Rachaad White, who are fantasy league average types that come at a reasonable cost. Considering the injury quotient at RB, that makes him a savvy investment.

So, how can the fantasy player exploit RPV?

By having a high-end RB1 and then drafting ANOTHER RB1 as your RB2, you have "frontloaded" the position and created an area of strength. That is one way to create an RPV advantage, but I prefer to use that same concept at WR in today's fantasy football world.

The BIGGEST mistake fantasy owners make in any sports in "filling their roster for positions," instead of filling their roster with talent and strength.

When you fill your roster for positions, you get a mediocre .500 team. When you fill your roster with strength, you have an advantage over the rest of the field. As long as you can responsibly fill the other positions and avoid Negative RPV as often as possible, that roster strength can carry your season.

With more NFL teams adapting backfield committees, the true starting running backs are worth more than ever in standard formats. That especially goes for the RB1s who get goal-line carries and the bulk of touches. In PPR, you can build the same strength of front-loading WR1s as you can with RB1s, then make up ground later by buying running backs in bulk with upside. The tough sell there is the difference between definitive running back touches as opposed to expected wide receiver catches. One is frankly more reliable on a weekly basis.

The same could be said for Superflex/2QB leagues. By "frontloading" elite QB play, you simultaneously create a team RPV strength and weaken the pool for the other owners. RPV shows you how stark the value can be position-to-position. Some will bottom out at -10% while others will be -20%. With middle-tier receivers, you'll see little advantage to be gained.

RPV is the ultimate tool to truly define talent and, even more importantly, where the drop-off in talent lies. Rankings are biased. RPV is honest.

Obviously, every league will be different. Flex players and OP (offensive player) slots will change values a bit, but the RPV theory holds in **EVERY LEAGUE and EVERY FORMAT**! It just needs to be adjusted according to each league's specifications. In the Black Book, I've done much of the work for you, but you must be sure to adjust the RPV for your league(s) quirky scoring wrinkles if you are going to truly achieve ultimate success.

Now that we've outlined RPV, let's dive deeper.

RPV IN PRACTICE (Draft and Trades)

Last year, so many folks asked, "How does the Black Book determine its RPV?"

The Black Book takes a combination of 3-year averages (when applicable/available), previous season stats, and the upcoming season projections, creating a hybrid point total for each player that then gets utilized within the RPV equation.

For rookies, clearly there is no track record from which to work to create that number. Therefore, I use a composite of projected stats from a few choice entities, their college statistical profile, and their potential use in their new team system in order to create each rookie's point total for the RPV formula.

With so many new styles of fantasy football, it's crucial to understand the value of each position in your league.

For example, I prefer PPR (point per reception) setups that play a lineup consisting of QB, RB, RB/WR, WR1, WR2, WR3, TE, K, 5 IDP and an OP slot (which can be a QB) or a second mandatory QB spot.

If a quarterback is the most important skills entity in *real* football, I want my fantasy experience to mirror that truth. The RPV for this kind of league is different than a standard league. Teams play 2 QBs every week, therefore QBs become the equivalent of the RB1/RB2 RPV I just laid out in the last section.

Another big adjustment: Since I technically only have to start 1 RB, the talent pool is adjusted back into a "one large group of running backs" theory. Possession WRs and big playmakers garner attention. This is a perfect example of why a tool like RPV is so necessary. If I were to use the standard old rankings from a website or a magazine in this format, I would get crushed.

Now more than ever, there is no "one ranking system" that will be useful to you in any format. Ignore these Top 100 lists and nonsense like that -- and instead focus on the true value and weight of the player in *your* league. That's why RPV works.

The last best thing about RPV is the fact it strips away a lot of the hype and noise surrounding the athletes, as well as the fictional computer projections that can be misleading and downright destructive.

RPV is about understanding a player's value -- his ACTUAL value. Not what his value may be projected to be while you sit in last place wondering where you went wrong. The best way to evaluate a player is through a mixture of career averages, previous statistics and projections that are then weighed against the other players of the same position. NOT PROJECTIONS ALONE!

Using only last year's numbers will give you a great team … for last season. Using just projections will give you a great team … in theory. RPV will give you a great team in REALITY!

You can choose to be great at one spot or two, but if you are below-average at other places, your overall RPV will even out. You may find yourself managing a middle-of-the-road team. Being above-average in as many places as you can, even without a top-flight star, you will find yourself consistently out-producing your opponents. If you use RPV correctly, you may even find yourself above average in most places and great in others, which makes you the one to beat. It's the ability to adapt, adjust and understand that separates us. RPV is the difference-maker.

RPV can tell you not only how much better a player is than the average for his position, but also how much better he is than the next guy available at his position on the draft board. Understanding these RPV relationships is key in maximizing your positional advantage.

To illustrate this point and its application, let's take a draft-day example. It's your turn to pick, and you have openings to fill at WR and TE. The top available players on the board at each position look like this:

WR

- Player A: +15% RPV
- Player B: +10% RPV
- Player C: +8% RPV
- Player D: +7% RPV
- Player E: +5% RPV

TE

- Player F: +8% RPV
- Player G: -2% RPV
- Player H: -2% RPV
- Player I: -4% RPV
- Player J: -6% RPV

At first glance, you might be inclined to take Player A, who is a +15% better than the average at his position. All other things being equal, however, Player F is probably the better choice.

Even though he is only +8% better than the average, the drop-off between him and the next-best player at his position is 10 percentage points. That's a significant dip. If you take Player A now, Player F almost definitely won't be on the board when your next pick rolls around, and at best you'll be stuck with an average or below-average tight end.

If you take Player F now, however, you'll be on the right side of that 10% RPV advantage over the teams who haven't drafted a TE yet. You'll also probably lose out on Player A at WR, but you will still most likely get someone from the above list (Player C, D or E) -- all of whom are trading in the same RPV range and, more importantly, still in the positive. It may not sound like a big deal with mere percentage points, but it adds up the more you rise above or fall below the average RPV threshold.

By picking this way, you end up with a strong advantage at one position while remaining above average at the other. The alternative is to be above-average at one position and decidedly average or worse at the other. That's the reason so many fantasy owners fail. Usually, they base these decisions on the *name* of the player instead of his Relative Position Value. The same can be said when evaluating trades. You must look at what advantage you're gaining and potentially losing in each deal.

The fantasy manager who does that effectively has a distinct advantage.

Remember, don't marginalize your strength!

Everyone has access to opinions, but now you have access to RPV.

Chapter 3

Draft Strategies 2024

Joe Pisapia

Draft Strategies

PPR League Strategy

	Round 1	Round 2	Round 3	Round 4
Team 1	CeeDee Lamb	Patrick Mahomes II	Travis Etienne Jr.	Tee Higgins
Team 2	Christian McCaffrey	Deebo Samuel Sr.	Mike Evans	Amari Cooper
Team 3	Tyreek Hill	Brandon Aiyuk	Sam LaPorta	Isiah Pacheco
Team 4	Ja'Marr Chase	Travis Kelce	Josh Allen	James Cook
Team 5	Justin Jefferson	Derrick Henry	Jalen Hurts	Keenan Allen
Team 6	Amon-Ra St. Brown	Chris Olave	Michael Pittman Jr.	Anthony Richardson
Team 7	A.J. Brown	Kyren Williams	Lamar Jackson	De'Von Achane
Team 8	Puka Nacua	Jahmyr Gibbs	Alvin Kamara	Stefon Diggs
Team 9	Garrett Wilson	Jonathan Taylor	Cooper Kupp	Josh Jacobs
Team 10	Breece Hall	Nico Collins	DJ Moore	Rachaad White
Team 11	Bijan Robinson	Davante Adams	Jaylen Waddle	DK Metcalf
Team 12	Saquon Barkley	Marvin Harrison Jr.	Drake London	Joe Mixon

In PPR leagues, I'm hitting wide receivers early and often. The top talent on the board is going to fly off fast and furious. When you enter the WR3 tier, the questions really start to grow regarding wide receivers outside of the top 30. 24+ WR will likely be gone in the first four rounds, so waiting on wideout is not an option. I'm all right with grabbing running backs at the "turn" of drafts with a first or second round pick, but not at the top or middle of the first as many ADPs on sites will suggest they be drafted. There are plenty of later running backs of interest being undervalued, such as Zamir White, Zack Moss, and James Conner slated for the bulk of the carries in their offenses. Lead wide receivers are long gone by then on the offenses you want to be invested in, and even late running back fliers like Jonathan Books and Kimani Vidal could make a second half season impact.

The elite-level QBs are worth the investment, but I would rather be at the tail end of that run instead of leading the charge. More than ever, these guys are winning you weeks and dominating even single-quarterback leagues. Should you miss that run, Anthony Richardson has great upside, or you can draft a safe Jordan Love later. If I had my choice, give me the top of the draft for an elite WR or middle of the draft for the underrated Amon-Ra St. Brown to start, and we're off to the races. Watch veterans like Cooper Kupp, Stefon Diggs, and Alvin Kamara. Those are three first round talents going later than usual. My money is on Kamara to be the best return on investment in 2024.

Superflex League Strategy

	Round 1	Round 2	Round 3	Round 4
Team 1	CeeDee Lamb	Justin Herbert	Kirk Cousins	Cooper Kupp
Team 2	Christian McCaffrey	Brock Purdy	Davante Adams	Baker Mayfield
Team 3	Tyreek Hill	Jordan Love	Jared Goff	Deebo Samuel Sr.
Team 4	Ja'Marr Chase	Kyler Murray	Marvin Harrison Jr.	Travis Etienne Jr.
Team 5	Justin Jefferson	Dak Prescott	Jonathan Taylor	Sam LaPorta
Team 6	Amon-Ra St. Brown	C.J. Stroud	Nico Collins	Derrick Henry
Team 7	Patrick Mahomes II	Garrett Wilson	Kyren Williams	Mike Evans
Team 8	Josh Allen	Puka Nacua	Jahmyr Gibbs	Jayden Daniels
Team 9	Jalen Hurts	Saquon Barkley	Caleb Williams	Drake London
Team 10	Lamar Jackson	Bijan Robinson	Travis Kelce	Michael Pittman Jr.
Team 11	Anthony Richardson	A.J. Brown	Chris Olave	Trevor Lawrence
Team 12	Breece Hall	Joe Burrow	Tua Tagovailoa	Brandon Aiyuk

Superflex, ahh the best of fantasy football formats! Every superflex league is going to be a bit of a poker game. Some managers will start taking quarterbacks right at 1.01 and start the run, some leagues will have more managers with the discipline to wait and let quarterbacks fall to the mid-first round range, which is really what should happen. Personally, I would love to grab a top WR before going quarterback, but that luxury isn't always afforded if you want a top 5 guy at QB. Last year, I warned there was a frightening abundance of rookies, second-year, and unproven quarterbacks that meant you had to hit the position early for any stability. I was right, and injuries compounded the issue of ineptitude.

This year, the rookie crop is far more intriguing for fantasy. Caleb Williams and Jayden Daniels specifically I expect to basically hit the ground running. They may struggle occasionally in reality, but fantasy productivity should be present regardless of the learning curve. In superflex drafts where quarterback runs happen early, remember that high-end skill players will get suppressed. Therefore, don't be afraid to either jump into the QB pool, or pile up on high-end skill players. Just make sure you don't miss out on the Kirk Cousins/Jared Goff types to at least solidify some basic floor of QB1 play.

Standard League Strategy

	Round 1	Round 2	Round 3	Round 4
Team 1	Christian McCaffrey	Davante Adams	Michael Pittman Jr.	Stefon Diggs
Team 2	CeeDee Lamb	Lamar Jackson	Travis Etienne Jr.	Tee Higgins
Team 3	Tyreek Hill	Patrick Mahomes II	Rachaad White	DeVonta Smith
Team 4	Ja'Marr Chase	Jalen Hurts	Joe Mixon	Amari Cooper
Team 5	Justin Jefferson	Josh Allen	Chris Olave	Josh Jacobs
Team 6	Amon-Ra St. Brown	Travis Kelce	Anthony Richardson	DK Metcalf
Team 7	Breece Hall	Nico Collins	Mike Evans	James Cook
Team 8	Bijan Robinson	Marvin Harrison Jr.	Drake London	Isiah Pacheco
Team 9	A.J. Brown	Kyren Williams	Deebo Samuel Sr.	De'Von Achane
Team 10	Jonathan Taylor	Garrett Wilson	Sam LaPorta	Jaylen Waddle
Team 11	Derrick Henry	Puka Nacua	Brandon Aiyuk	Alvin Kamara
Team 12	Saquon Barkley	Jahmyr Gibbs	DJ Moore	Cooper Kupp

Standard leagues are about controlling players that control fantasy scoring in their offenses. Josh Allen and Jalen Hurts are either throwing or rushing in touchdowns, so they become extremely valuable, as does Anthony Richardson potentially. In standard formats (or even .5 PPR leagues), touchdown equity matters more. However, yards are still yards, and running backs have a bad habit of getting hurt. Therefore, those elite wide receivers are still top-tier investments in the format. I'd rather build from the best players available, rather than become too running back-centric.

I understand that standard leagues were once indeed the "standard" but playing in at least a .5 point PPR format is more advised. The game has evolved as has fantasy football along with it. Twenty years ago, there were plenty of bell bow backs running amuck and worthy of first round fantasy picks. It's just not where the game is right now. If you insist on keeping it old school, at least understand the old school approach of heavy running backs is outdated. Invest in good offenses in the "E.C.O." System, and look for offenses that funnel through certain players, and draft those specific guys as often as you can. That will give you a higher weekly floor compared to your league mates.

Salary Cap League Strategy

For Salary Cap leagues (auction style drafts), **I have built-in prices for the players next to the RPV in each position overview chapter**. These are merely guidelines, and these drafts tend to be all over the board in terms of value. I recommend a few things to stay steady in the midst of the chaos. First, get the players you really want, within reason. Don't overpay to an obscene amount, but remember, the draft is about acquiring talent. The waiver wire and trades can always help with depth, but once the great-impact players are gone, they're gone. Second, have pivot points for players. RPV is a great help with this because you can see the players who move the needle and the ones who don't. If you like a player, but the hype on him causes his price to climb, then have 2-4 pivot players that can give you similar stat lines. Paying a premium for elite talent is fine. Overpaying for mid-level talent can crush your season. Lastly, early in drafts, nominate players you don't want on your roster, especially pricey ones. That will drain money out of the room quicker and leave less cash on hand for other managers to bid against you for teh top guys you want to roster.

Guillotine League Strategy

For those unaware, Guillotine Leagues are fun, and you should try one. Basically, you draft, and every week, the lowest-scoring team gets cut from the league. Then, all the players from the cut team become free agents. I've personally had a fair amount of success with being reasonably aggressive on free agents. That means if there's a game-changing round one talent, I will be ultra-aggressive with my FAAB budget to acquire them. I'd also highly recommend combing the wire post waiver wire run for other players left or dropped, picking good talent up on the cheap, and stashing them on your bench. This may be tedious, but it will serve you well in the long run. Remember, the longer you last in this format, the less competition for free agents you will have and the cheaper good talent becomes. But that's only if you are still alive in the league to claim it, so play every week like it's your last and hope that you can get through the bye weeks. By the way, looking ahead on bye weeks and utilizing your bench in preparation for them is a great way to get an advantage over your opponents.

Best Ball League Strategy

For me, Best Ball strategy doesn't change all that much. However, here are a few things worthy of note. Top-level quarterbacks are going much higher than they were a few years ago. I think the "Hero RB Strategy", where you draft one true RB1 somewhat early then let the position come to you, building volume and upside at running back as the draft goes on, is a good way to mitigate risk, build a strong wide receiver group and ultimately put your team in a better place to succeed. Like all drafts, there will be ebbs, flows, and runs. The trick is to really focus on players from teams with good "E.C.O." Systems, especially late in these deep format drafts. If those players get opportunities, they could shine. Look at Puka Nakua from last year as a prime example of just how bright!

Chapter 4

Quarterback Profiles

Joe Pisapia

	SINGLE QB LEAGUE	RPV	$		QB2 SUPERFLEX	RPV
	Player				Player	
1	Patrick Mahomes II	14%	25	13	Kirk Cousins	10%
2	Josh Allen	11%	23	14	Justin Herbert	10%
3	Jalen Hurts	5%	22	15	Tua Tagovailoa	8%
4	Lamar Jackson	2%	16	16	Trevor Lawrence	6%
5	Joe Burrow	1%	10	17	Caleb Williams	6%
6	Anthony Richardson	1%	10	18	Jayden Daniels	4%
7	Dak Prescott	0%	9	19	Baker Mayfield	1%
8	Jordan Love	-2%	7	20	Matthew Stafford	-7%
9	C.J. Stroud	-3%	6	21	Aaron Rodgers	-8%
10	Brock Purdy	-9%	5	22	Geno Smith	-8%
11	Kyler Murray	-9%	5	23	Derek Carr	-10%
12	Jared Goff	-11%	4	24	Deshaun Watson	-12%

***Get updated RPV Cheat Sheets 10 & 12 tm leagues for one time $5 cost (free updates) PayPal: FantasyBlackBook@gmail.com or Venmo: @FantasyBlackBook
And include your email address***

Last year, I warned that the quarterback position was in serious peril considering the amount of inexperience under center in 2023. There were lots of rookies, second-year and first time starters, not to mention volatile situations like Deshaun Watson and advanced age of players like Aaron Rodgers. Heading into 2024, the pool will once again feature its fair share of young QBs, but the middle is far more comfortable, and the bottom of the position has the upside of youth like Drake Maye and J.J. McCarthy taking over at some point. There are also fewer true "battles" on the horizon, outside of possibly Russell Wilson/Justin Fields in Pittsburgh, no matter what Mike Tomlin tells the media.

The incredible amount of injuries at the position the last two years has led to an off-season of NFL GMs investing in higher quality backups. That also helps a great deal in superflex formats. 84 quarterbacks took a snap for NFL teams in 2023. That turnover not only hurt the QB position but also collective offenses that struggled with rhythm and execution. Luckily, there are plenty of values to be had, such as Kirk Cousins and Jared Goff if you don't want to chase the elite with early picks. Therefore, you have more leeway to approach superflex drafts with different strategies in '24, as opposed to the "get top QB early and often" approach I preached last year.

In single quarterback leagues, the top 10 is very strong, but the elite rushing quarterbacks are still a big advantage. The good news is that you can easily draft a safe Brock Purdy type late and then select a Caleb Williams or Jayden Daniels for upside with an even later pick and have the best of both worlds. Often drafting a second QB of note has become a good investment with the myriad of injuries at the position of late.

The Elite

1. **Patrick Mahomes, KC:** The Chiefs did not make it easy for Patrick Mahomes last year. His receiver room was a hot mess. Kadarius Toney couldn't catch a ball, Skyy Moore couldn't run the right route, and Travis Kelce was banged up most of the year. Rashee Rice emerged as the "go-to" guy and red zone target in the second half, but now he faces league suspension for an off-season reckless driving incident. For perspective, Mahomes had just (4) 300-yard games last year. The season before, he had 10! Kelce signed a two-year extension, Hollywood Brown was brought in, and speedster Xavier Worthy was drafted at the end of the first round of the draft. Mahomes is the best real life QB in the game, but he could be lined up to become the best fantasy QB again in 2024. In '23, his 4.1K passing yards and 27 TDs were a far cry from the usual 5K and 40 TD ceiling that Mahomes flirts with annually. The good news is that the down year could make him slightly cheaper in single QB league drafts this year. I'm not a fan of Matt Nagy's play calling, but it was clear the receivers were the issue in '23 more than anything. A healthy Kelce and the normal KC continuity make Mahomes one of the most investable assets in fantasy in any format.

2. **Josh Allen, BUF:** Despite the disintegration of Stefon Diggs in the latter part of 2023, Josh Allen still ascended to the number one QB in fantasy. Allen threw for 4.3K yards and 29 TDs. He also rushed for a whopping more TDs, more than double his previous season total. Allen did struggle at times on the road where his QBR dipped and his INT% rose. Keon Coleman was the big weapon drafted, but no one on this team can replace a prime version of Diggs. Now, it will come down to the development of Dalton Kincaid and Khalil Shakir and the ability of Josh Allen to simply find the open man rather than force feeding targets to one alpha WR. All of the above could take some time to manifest, but in the meantime, Allen offers a very high floor of rushing and passing equity. One note: his 18 INTs were a career-high, but 3 of them came in Week 1 against the Jets, so let's not overreact to that number and hope that Allen can now take the next step in his career, which is seeing the field at a higher level. Despite Stefon Diggs's disappointing second half, his presence opened up a lot in the offense. His removal from it, even if his prime was over, leaves some questions for Allen and the Bills offense. Add in the high INT rate and unproven weapons, and Allen may fall short of the #1 QB in fantasy two years in a row.

3. **Jalen Hurts, PHI:** Not to be outdone by Josh Allen, Jalen Hurts also had a record-setting 15 TDs in 2023. Now, many were due to the famous "Brotherly Shove," but with Jason Kelce retiring, one has to wonder if that will be as easy for the Eagles in '24. Regardless, Hurts should be good for 600+ rushing yards, and he

still has top-tier weapons to work with A.J. Brown, DeVonta Smith, and hopefully a healthier Dallas Goedert. He will also now have a true star running back for the first time in Saquon Barkley, who comes to the division rival Eagles with a chip on his shoulder. The addition of Barkley could also eat into that grand rushing TD total but coming off a career-high 3.8K passing yards, Barkley could also help push that number for 4K for the first time with his YAC ability. Hurts threw for a career-high 23 TDs, but he also had a high in INTs (15). The Eagles had a bear of a schedule last year and really wore down mentally and physically last year. With leadership lacking on offense with Kelce gone, Hurts will have an opportunity to take his game to the next level. How he bounces back from the adversity of last season will be interesting to see, but in fantasy terms, he's lined up to be an elite option. He will also have yet another play caller now, which he's had for almost every season of his pro and college career. Yikes. I would not reach for him over Lamar Jackson or Patrick Mahomes with my draft capital, but he's a superflex first-round pick.

4. **Lamar Jackson, BAL:** Lamar Jackson won his second MVP last year, despite the fact there were 6 games where Jackson did not finish as a QB1 in fantasy. His 821 rushing yards were the most since his 2020 campaign. He threw for a career-high 3.6K passing yards, 24 TDs, and rushed for another 5 TDs. Basically, Jackson carried the Ravens offense. His wide receiver play was inconsistent again, and Mark Andrews missed time for a second straight season. This offseason, Derrick Henry was brought in, but I don't think that will impact Jackson's rushing touchdown equity all that much. Zay Flowers is his best WR option, but he will need to take a step forward in year two as the rest of this group (Rashod Bateman, Nelson Agholor) is suspect. If Mark Andrews should miss time again, Isaiah Likely should once again step in and not miss a beat. The Ravens will be back to their running ways in 2024, but if 3.5K yards passing and 800 rushing yards is the new Lamar floor, he's going to win you a lot of matchups in 2024.

The Wild Card

1. **Anthony Richardson, IND:** We received a mere taste of Anthony Richardson last year, and we're all hungry for more. His rocket arm, linebacker size, and running back speed make him a candidate to break the fantasy wheel at the QB position. He's also in the right place with HC Shane Steichen, who is one of the best young coaches and offensive minds in the game. The shoulder injury that cut his 2023 short should not be an issue heading into training camp. If he stays healthy, 3.5K yards passing and 600 yards rushing is well within his reach. There may be some peaks and valleys, as Richardson is still very raw and barely played 3 games last season. But in those games, Richardson had 21.9 points (QB4) fantasy points in Week 1 and 29.6 points (QB2) in Week 4. Michael Pittman Jr. is a very underrated #1 target, rookie Adonai Mitchell is a field stretcher, and a healthy Jonathan Taylor is enough to make the Colts a potential playoff team. The future is very exciting, and Richardson is a first-round pick in dynasty and superflex formats. In single QB formats, I would draft him once the established elite tier starts coming off the board.

Top Talent

1. **C.J. Stroud, HOU:** My number 1 rookie QB of 2023 over-delivered on even my high expectations. The reigning Offensive Rookie of the Year will now have the pressure of living up to expectations. Personally, I think Stroud is up for the task. He should easily cross 4K yards passing again and should raise his 23 TD mark as well. He threw just 5 INTs in '23, and that was a big reason for his success. Nico Collins is a star, Stefon Diggs was brought in and may be better suited to a #2 receiver role at this stage of his career. Tank Dell was explosive before his injury, and now veteran Joe Mixon brings stability to the backfield. Perhaps most impressive was Stroud's quality play despite the offensive line injuries in the first half. Because rushing isn't his game, you need that O-line to stay healthy in 2024, and Stroud needs to maintain something close to his pace of 273 YPG (3rd in NFL) that he posted last year. The Texans have surrounded him with enough help to be confident Stroud can at least maintain, if not improve, his fantasy numbers in 2024.

2. **Joe Burrow, CIN:** Joe Burrow looks healthy in workouts right now, and there's no question when he is healthy, Burrow is a top-tier QB in the league. In four seasons, he's played 16 games twice and 10 games twice. Regardless, Borrow's stats are very consistent when under center, and in his full seasons, it's easy to expect 4.5+K passing yards and 35 TDs. Burrow still has all world Ja'Marr Chase to work with, and the sneaky upside draft pick of Jermaine Burton gives the offense some depth of playmaking ability. The team has continued to spend on offensive line help including Trent Brown this off-season. Protection for Burrow has been an issue in the past, and while this current lot isn't elite, it's a top 15 unit. Burrow is set to be a strong single QB league value, but he won't give you much rushing equity, so if you're looking for a "league winner" type, I'd push more toward Anthony Richardson. However, Burrow is easily C.J. Stroud's equal (if not better), so if you're looking for steady fantasy QB play, a cheaper Burrow is a better investment.

3. **Dak Prescott, DAL:** Well Dak Prescott finally started forcing the ball to CeeDee Lamb, and wouldn't you know it, the Cowboys passing attack improved! Prescott led the league with 36 TDs with just 9 INTs and 4.5K passing yards. His 410 completions were also a league-best, and considering the running back room in Dallas may be worse than it was last year, I would expect him to be near the league leaders in attempts and completions again in 2024. The Cowboys' lack of balance is a win for fantasy managers, so Prescott should again be a very solid mid-tier QB1 this season. The only thing that could seriously derail Prescott's value would be a CeeDee Lamb injury. That would be devastating. The irony with Dak is that Cowboy fans have contempt for him, and that negativity seems to follow him unfairly into his general public perception. That rings true in fantasy as well, which makes Dak a surprising value in superflex formats.

4. **Kyler Murray, ARI:** Recovery from knee surgery delayed Kyler Murray's 2023 season debut. Over the 8 games he did play, he often flirted with low-end QB1 fantasy value. Rather than try and glean too much from last year's incomplete report card, it would be more practical to lean on projections when it comes to Murray specifically more than most other quarterbacks. Murray now has a true alpha dog WR in Marvin Harrison Jr., who will make one heck of a tandem threat with TE Trey McBride. The Cardinals offensive line is still subpar at best, but you can look at that two ways. On one hand, that means Murray is out in space running for yards and TDs, making fantasy points. On the other, lack of protection could lead to more injuries to Murray. The Cardinals did have a nice draft and seem to be turning a corner as a roster. Trey Benson offers them some much-needed depth at running back and balance will be a key for this offense in '24. My expectations for Murray are 3.5K passing yards, 500 rushing yards, and 27 total TDs (pass & rush). Yes, there is risk, but 17 games played should equate to a top 10 QB finish for Murray.

Solid Options

1. **Jordan Love, GB:** A lackluster start to Love's starting role gave way to an elite-level second half. Over his last eight games, Love averaged 268.8 passing yards per game, with 18 TDs, and just 1 INT. What made this run so impressive was the fact he was doing it with Jayden Reed and Romeo Dobbs as Christian Watson seemed to always be dealing with an injury. The Packers were also the youngest team in the NFL last year, so if this is the new established baseline, they could become a real force in the NFC for the next decade. I like that they brought in Josh Jacobs and drafted Marshawn Lloyd because a balanced offense will continue to let Love see honest looks from defenses and place him ultimately in a place to succeed. It would be safe to say that Love's dominant finish was surprising and that's why I have him just shy of the "Top Talent" tier. If he drops 4.2K passing yards and 30+ TDs again, he'll cement himself as a top fantasy guy. That late-season run also included opponents like the Giants, Chargers, Bears, Vikings (with no QB), and the Panthers. After a tremendous playoff run, that schedule will be tougher in 2024, and Love will have to step up to meet the challenge.

2. **Brock Purdy, SF:** Statistically, Brock Purdy and Jordan Love were nearly identical. Purdy could be selected over Love based simply upon the weapons and public footprint of the 49ers. However, Purdy is more reliant on the talent around him than Love and, therefore, behind him in my rankings. In games where Purdy was missing Christian McCaffrey or other offensive pieces, there were some struggles. Week 6 against CLE, for example, was a QB25 finish, and the following week in MIN, he was QB16. Let's also not forget that 4 INT performance at home against the Ravens (that was ugly). Regardless, he still finished as QB7 in scoring last year and should be drafted as a QB1, but he remains the kind of fantasy QB that I would want to use draft capital on some insurance on with a backup on my roster. 4K passing yards and 28 TDs seem like a strong projection to base his value on, but I can't shake quite yet the Cinderella story having a dark turn. Yet.

3. **Tua Tagovailoa, MIA:** Tua was the anti-Jordan Love last year. He started out gangbusters with serious MVP buzz. Over the first eight games, he averaged more than 300 YPG and was QB5. Then, the bottom fell out for him, and he was QB20 from Week 9 to the finish. So, who is the REAL Tua? Well, on the plus side, he runs the fastest offense on the planet led by one of the craftiest play callers in Mike McDaniel. The efficiency was there last year. Miami was middle of the pack with 566 Pass Att, but second in the league with 4,698 passing yards. Let's be honest here, Tyreek Hill, Jaylen Waddle, and his speedy cohorts make Tua shine. I find it mildly concerning that he slimmed down this off-season because his smaller frame has led to injury concerns in the past. His 4.6K passing yards and 29 TD/14 INT line was the best of his career. If he's going to make that the "new benchmark" he'll need Hill and Waddle to both stay healthy and that was tricky at times in 2023. He'll likely be right at the bubble of QB1/QB2 in many drafts. In superflex leagues he's a nice double-up with a Jared Goff or Kirk Cousins steady type QB2. In single QB leagues, I prefer to be more proactive and aggressive with some of the game-changers ahead of him or wait longer and play the hot hand with a veteran and an upside youngster.

4. **Jared Goff, DET:** Most people won't get excited when they draft Jared Goff, but those people don't appreciate the QB7 in fantasy last year. Goff averaged 17.8 FPPG last year which was right at the QB1/QB2 level with QBs that played full seasons. He has one of the most underappreciated assets in Amon-Ra St. Brown, and the second half rocket ship that was Jahmyr Gibbs means the Lions can be even more explosive in 2024. There may not be much room to grow for Goff, but we'd all gladly sign up for a repeat of 4.5K yards and 30 TDs again in 2024. We know what he is, and that's a pocket passer for an NFC contender and someone who finally seems to have settled into his strengths and cleaned up his weaknesses. He's a valuable superflex quarterback, and in any salary cap format, he'll be a surprisingly good return on a reasonable investment.

5. **Justin Herbert, LAC:** Did you know Justin Herbert averaged 18.5 FPPG last year? That was 11th best in fantasy. So, why is everyone all of a sudden out on the boy wonder who was a fantasy darling just a year ago? Because people lack vision. Justin Herbest lost his safety blanket, Keenan Allen, but he gained a real football coach in Jim Harbaugh, fresh off an NCAA National Championship at Michigan. Harbaugh played QB in the NFL at a high level and Herbert now has the benefit of developing under someone who truly can take him to the next level. Yes, Harbaugh and OC Greg Roman will want to run the football (a lot), but that doesn't mean Herbert's fantasy value is gone. I love the Georgia WR Ladd McConkey they drafted, who could easily step in immediately and lead the team in targets. Josh Palmer is league average and then there's the enigma that is Quentin Johnston. If Harbaugh was smart, and I believe he is, he'll cater to Johnston's strengths, which beat his Wolverines in the college playoff a few years ago and throw him screens all day. Herbert's broken finger that cost him the final four games of the season shouldn't be an issue. There's a world where Herbert is the most poorly ranked QB by the fantasy community at large and could blow well past his ADP. The worst case scenario is the now run-heavy Chargers limit him to his current early QB2 ADP. Both scenarios work for me and so does Herbert.

6. **Kirk Cousins, ATL:** The QB7 in FPPG (19.4) is now on his third organization. Kirk Cousins is coming off a season-ending Achilles injury and finds himself in a new Falcons offense with some high-octane young

talent. It could very well take some time for Cousins to harness the best out of this group. Having Drake London, Kyle Pitts, and Bijan Robinson puts Cousins in another strong scenario to succeed, and it was downright infuriating to watch that trio struggle with abysmal quarterback play last year. As usual, Cousins is being criminally undervalued, QB18 in some early consensus ranks. That's ridiculous. He has three straight years of 4K passing yards and 29+ TDs. Sure, he had Justin Jefferson in Minnesota, but he has plenty of toys in Atlanta. I'd be thrilled with some combination in superflex of Cousins/Purdy/Daniels/Goff. In deeper leagues, if you wait on QB Cousins remains a safe investment despite the new learning curve facing him in Atlanta. Patience will be rewarded, though, just don't freak out in September if the offense is a work in progress.

7. **Trevor Lawrence, JAC:** Trevor Lawrence was QB13 last year but QB17 in FPPG (17.3). Sure, the best ability sometimes is availability, but Lawrence's 2023 was disappointing compared to expectations. His strong sophomore season under Doug Pederson and the acquisition of Calvin Ridley set some high expectations but ultimately under-delivered. His passing yard total, TDs, and INT all regressed. In fact, his 21 TD/14 INT were downright troublesome. Lawrence is still just 24 and has Christian Kirk as the "go-to guy", Evan Engram, and Travis Etienne. They brought in the enigmatic Gabe Davis and drafted Brian Thomas Jr. from LSU. All of this doesn't make me feel great about 2024, but Lawrence is young enough to continue to develop, and the pedigree is too high to dismiss at this stage. He's not an ideal QB1 in single QB leagues (even deeper ones). As a QB2, you could do worse, and he may be an interesting buy low in keeper/dynasty formats.

Up and Coming

1. **Caleb Williams, CHI:** Caleb Williams ticks all the boxes. Great arm, incredible improvisational ability, mobility, and a knack for big plays. Although, in theory, having D.J. Moore and Keenan Allen should allow Williams to hit the ground running, I can't help but ponder the environment he'll be in with the Bears. It's a cold physical environment for the USC guy, it's a very tough fan base to win over and extremely vocal when disappointed, and most importantly, the coaching staff is not what I would roll out as my ideal scenario to develop a franchise quarterback. Williams' extension of plays led to some great highlights but also 32 fumbles in 25 games. That will kill him at this level. His ceiling is still the highest of this rookie class. In single QB redraft leagues, I am willing to pass more proven entities such as Brock Purdy or Justin Herbert. In superflex, Williams is a more intriguing lottery ticket. Can he be the first Bears QB to throw for 4K yards and 30 TDs? Maybe. Do I want to pay a premium to find out? I don't. Still, in dynasty leagues, Williams' long-term projectability makes him a premium asset, you just have to recognize there are some negatives that could hold him back from reaching his full potential.

2. **Jayden Daniels, WAS:** Jayden Daniels will be cheaper in every draft than Caleb Williams and may very well outscore him in 2024. The reason: his incredible rushing ability. Now, in the NFL, he better learn to slide more and live to fight another day or he'll end up getting crushed and missing time. Arm strength and touch are there, as are questions of blooming late in his college career. Joe Burrow faced similar shots, and things worked out alright for that LSU kid. The facts are Daniels has undeniable fantasy upside, and Washington, with second-time-around HC Dan Quinn, gives me reason for optimism. Could he throw for 3.5K yards and rush for 600+K in year one? Yeah, I think this Heisman winner can, and that's why, in superflex, I'd rather take him at a cheaper cost of Caleb Williams and his inflation rate.

3. **Drake Maye, NE:** The Patriots finally have their quarterback of the future after the failed Cam Newton experiment and flier on Mac Jones. Now, New England did neither of those two favors with atrocious offensive play calling and a lack of impact weapons. Sadly, Drake Maye seems to be in a similar bind. New OC Alex Van Pelt at least has some 'cache' as a former backup QB in the league, and working with Zac Taylor and Kevin Stefanski's offenses in various roles. However, he doesn't have a lot of play-calling experience. Back to Drake Maye. He's more of a Philip Rivers/Carson Palmer type pocket passer with a big arm. Most scouts agree, his footwork needs to be cleaned up, but that's something you can fix. Arm strength is a gift, and he has it. Will he start Week 1? I think it's more likely we get an October debut from May, and Jacoby Brissett runs this team for the first month and change of the season. Long term, Maye should become a solid mid-low end QB1 in fantasy over time IF the Patriots smarten up and give him some weapons to work with as his career unfolds. If they continue to fail in that regard as they have in years past, Maye will have a harder time ultimately finding success with the Patriots.

4. **J.J. McCarthy MIN:** The leader of the NCAA National Champs wasn't always asked to carry the burden of the Michigan offense, with a run-heavy scheme. However, you can't deny McCarthy has that intangible winning mentality that's taken him from high school success into college success. McCarthy landed in Minnesota, potentially the most coveted rookie QB landing place with the all-world Justin Jefferson and a great offensive mind in HC Kevin O'Connell. Now, we play the waiting game. Sam Darnold was brought in to bridge the gap, but McCarthy will be knocking on the door sooner than later. Arm strength is not an issue, but he does need to keep making progress with his second and third reads, which he began in 2023 at Michigan. Winning the job outright in 2024 seems unlikely to me and possibly counterproductive for the long haul development of J.J., yet it would not be shocking to see the guy who just finds ways to win, do it again.

5. **Bo Nix, DEN:** It was really hard for me to shake the many years of watching Bo Nix founder in the SEC with Auburn. He was bloodline royalty there, but eventually became the jester. He then goes to Oregan, dropped behind a massive offensive line in a weaker conference and goes in round one to Sean Payton and the Denver Broncos. I have long heralded Payton as one of the great coaches of QBs the NFL has seen in this generation, but I think he has his work cut out for him here. I know he threw 45 TDs last year and just 3 INT at Oregon last year, but so much success came from the unique (and highly efficient) Oregon offensive system. Could Payton shape his offense and lean into what was working for Nix so well last year? He better, because if he expects him to become a reliable starter in the NFL I'm skeptical there's another pathway to get there.

6. **Michael Penix, ATL:** Michael Penix had a great 2023 college season. He has a penchant for big plays and is not afraid to play gunslinger in big spots. Sure, he didn't get his fairy tale college ending, but you couldn't deny the raw tools of Penix after his finals season at Washington. There are some accuracy questions and now he's buried behind Kirk Cousins for the foreseeable future. Not to mention, he's on the older side for a prospect. Theoretically, Penix could end up sliding into a ready-made spot if Cousins turns this talented offense around and gets them on the right track. He could also be thrust into a starting role before he's ready due to an injury. Or he could find himself being forgotten over time on the depth chart. It's the numerous range of outcomes that makes Penix an enigma in fantasy. 2024 values seems nil, long term seems cloudy. I still like the player, it's just tough to see return on investment potential.

7. **Spencer Rattler, NO:** Once upon a time, Spencer Rattler was supposed to be the Gold Child of QB prospects, but after being replaced by Oklahoma HC Lincoln Riley with Caleb WIlliams, Rattler journeyed to South Carolina where the O-Line did him no favors. There's raw talent here, the question is, can someone harness it at the NFL level and develop him? The jury remains out on that one. However, he's a dynasty stash on the QB depth chart just in case for now.

Upside Play

1. **Justin Fields, PIT:** If you miss out on Anthony Richardson in a superflex league, Justin Fields is a very interesting flier. He's only a year removed from a 1K yard rushing season. He was also QB13 in FPPG (18.4), and the only thing standing in his way is Russell Wilson. Sure, Mike Tomlin is holding steadfast that Wilson is his starter, which makes sense as he has the more accomplished resume'. However, if they loved Wilson so much, then why did they acquire Fields in the first place this off-season? Exactly. Fields certainly has failed to make the most of his abilities at the NFL level, but the Bears were a hot mess as was his offensive line most of his career in Chicago. Pittsburgh, on the other hand, is a pillar of NFL stability, having three coaches since 1969. It may take an injury or some losses, or further decline in Russell Wilson, but Fields could see time as a starter in 2024, and that makes him the most desirable third QB on any superflex roster. I'd also be buying in dynasty leagues on Fields, too, based on his age and athleticism.

Serviceable Veterans

1. **Baker Mayfield, TB:** I will readily admit, I was not bullish when it came to Baker Mayfield last year, and I was happily proved wrong. OC Dave Canales was able to harness all the best qualities of Baker Mayfield and somehow turned him into a very steady league average (dare I say dependable?) quarterback. The trouble is Canales left for the Carolina HC job and Liam Coen now takes over play calling. Still, I'm cautiously optimistic based on 2023's career high in passing yards (first time over 4K) and TDs (28). Perhaps most encouraging, was Mayfield's mere 10 INTs. Historically, Mayfield's gunslinger mentality wrote too many checks he couldn't cash. Mike Evans and Chris Godwin remain, as does Rachad White, so stability of roster is another win for Baker. He's a decent QB2 in superflex and hopefully he can build on his strong 2023 finish (4 of his last 6 games he had 2 or more TDs)

2. **Matthew Stafford, LAR:** With a young Rams team and very little expectations, Matthew Stafford turned in a solid season at the age of 36. Back issues and other ailments have hampered him of late, so it was nice to see Stafford back under center looking his old self more often than not. The physical issues still make him risky, but Sean McVay remains a genius and Puka Nakua was nothing short of a fantasy revelation. Cooper Kupp also has a lot of tread on his tires, but if he and Nakua, Stafford should once again make a run at 4L passing yards and 25+ TDs which makes him a decent low-end QB2 in superflex. Chasing 2021's 41 TD season is folly but Stafford still has some decent low-key fantasy value, and the fact he's a boring veteran will keep his price low.

3. **Aaron Rodgers, NYJ:** A comical end at the beginning of the 2023 season left huge questions surrounding Aaron Rodgers. Sure, he's had a Hall of Fame career, but last season I warned of his age and decline throughout his numbers in his final season with the Packers. Garret Wilson is a fantastic WR1 who has yet to have the benefit of anything resembling good quarterback play. Mike Williams is always hurt and seems like the worst guy to play on the much-maligned MetLife Stadium turf. Breece Hall will be leaned on heavily and in theory, a healthy Aaron Rodgers is a low-end QB2 in sueprflex. To think he's anything more than that would be delusional...like, darkness retreat, ayahuasca level delusions.

4. **Geno Smith, SEA:** But 2022 was so fun! Alas, 2023 saw Geno Smith regress. Ironically Dave Canelas (who fixed Baker Mayfield last year), left for Tampa Bay last year and Geno Smith took a step backward. New HC Mike Macdonald says Geno is his starter, but they did bring in Sam Howell as a young, upside backup. Smith went from 4.2K yards to 3.6K, 30 TDs to just 20, and it's not like he didn't have the same cast of characters around him. He had D.K. Metcalf, Tyler Lockett and even rookie Jaxon Smith-Njigba. Everyone is returning for 2024, except Pette Carroll of course, so if Geno can find a middle ground between '22 and '23 he'd be a serviceable, low end QB2 in fantasy. Maybe we can chalk up last year's disappointment to the pressure of the new contract he signed last off-season.

5. **Derek Carr, NO:** Derek Carr threw for 3.8K yards, 25 TDs, and 8 INT. He also took a pounding behind a bad offensive line. At this point, Carr is a low-end QB2 who still has some strong weapons like Alvin Kamara and Chsi Olave around him. My big worry, though, is that butt-kicking he took physically week in and out in '23 carrying over to this season. Hopefully, rookie Taliese Fuaga at LT can help alleviate my concerns. If the line play improves, Carr could cross the 4K passing yard mark again.

Red Flags

1. **Daniel Jones, NYG:** Hey, guess what!? It's another "prove it year" for Daniel Jones. His 700 rushing yards in '22 piqued the interest of the fantasy community last year, but that turned out to be a big letdown. He was limited to just 6 games, and he had just 2 TDs and 6 INTs in those contests. The offensive line is still suspect and despite drafting Malik Nabers as the true alpha WR, Jones has never been a prolific passer in the NFL. His high watermark was 3.2K in '22. The Giants are financially committed to Jones, and he remains a low-end QB2 with rushing upside. It just feels like we're in this same cycle as the Giants, where we're waiting for everything to click but it never quite does. Losing Saquon Barkley also hurts. His numbers without Barkley have always been significantly worse than with him. There always seems to be an excuse made for Jones' shortcomings. Maybe, it's time to stop making excuses and blame Jones?

2. **Bryce Young, CAR:** I had massive concerns about the size of Bryce Young and the landing spot, and so far, I've been validated. With a great O-line and weapons, Young could be a capable facilitator of the football, especially with new HC Dave Canales, who turned around Geno Smith and Baker Mayfield in back-to-back years. Now, those guys had D.K. Metcalf, Tyler Lockett, Mike Evans and Chris Godwin. Young has Diontae Johns, Adam Theilen and Xavier Leggette. What I am excited about is the prospect of running back Jonathan Brooks who could be a game changer for this offense as the season progresses. He would open up more play-action and keep defenses honest. I ultimately think Young will improve on his ghastly rookie season where he threw for just 10 TDs, 11 INTs and only 2.8K yards. However, I'm skeptical he can make a big enough jump in 2024 to make him a viable fantasy asset.

3. **Deshaun Watson, CLE:** In what seemingly feels like one of the biggest blunders in NFL front office history, Deshaun Watson's tenure as a Brown seems doomed. Controversies, injuries and bad play have become his M.O., and it doesn't feel as though the ship is ever going to correct course. There may be a better chance of Watson leaving Cleveland next year, than the starter in 2025. Still, in 2024 the Browns are stuck with Waston. His epic 2020 seems like a distant memory, a white whale fantasy managers will continue to chase, only to drown in a sea of...well...brown (if you know what I mean). Jameis Winston was brought in as the backup and patience will be thin with Waston in year three. If he isn't healthy or playing well, Winston will receive playing time.

4. **Russell Wilson, PIT:** The Russell Wilson feel-good Steeler vibes were short-lived. No sooner did he arrive in Steel City than the Steelers brought in completion in the form of Justin Fields. Fields is younger, faster, and comes with a high pedigree despite floundering in Chicago. Wilson is on a one-year deal, so he either balls out right out of the gate, or he'll be on the bench by Week 6. He's on a steady four-year decline statistically and I, for one, would be shocked to see him as the starter for Pittsburgh for 17 games. If he gets half that many under his belt, I'll be impressed. It's just not a great situation and new OC Arthur Smith is not a QB-friendly play caller.

5. **Will Levis, TEN**: In the interest of "keeping it real" I don't believe in Will Levis. I was not impressed by the college tape, nor surprised when he fell to the second round of the draft. Last year, he had one shiny game, and was basically a hot mess after that. Once the tape was out, defenses knew what to do. Yes, he does have arm strength and some improved theoretical weapons now that Calvin Ridley and Tyler Boyd have joined DeAndre Hopkins there. If those veterans stay healthy, Levis could reach his ceiling of a mid-range QB2. Frankly, I'm not buying it, nor am I buying the offensive line, which will not do him any favors. Too many new elements, including a new HC and system. Too much can go wrong.

6. **Sam Darnold, MIN:** Sam Darnold finds himself in a fascinating spot with one of the most gifted wide receivers on the planet in Justin Jefferson. The only trouble is, J.J. McCarthy was selected by the Vikings in the first round and expectations are that he takes over at some point this season. Darnold would have to fight him off in preseason and training camp to win the job AND get off to a hot start to hold the job. The former seems possible, the latter more unlikely. Darnold is still just 26, but he already seems like a journeyman. Darnold is unlikely to be a fantasy commodity.

7. **Gardner Minshew/Aiden O'Connell, LV:** Gardner Minshew did take the Colts to the playoffs last year, but he's still better suited to be a high-end backup as opposed to a weekly starter. His weaknesses always seem to get exposed the longer he plays. Aiden O'Connell did seem to get better as the year progressed. In three of his final four games, O'Connell has 240+ yards and 2+ TDs. Then the other was the horrendous Chiefs game where he threw for 62 yards (gulp). This figures to be a true QB battle throughout camp and neither is more than a bye week superflex QB play. Drafting both as your #2 QB in that format is a strategy, but not necessarily a successful one.

Chapter 5

Running Back Profiles

Derek Brown

	RB 1 PPR	RPV	$
1	Christian McCaffrey	22%	68
2	Bijan Robinson	12%	55
3	Breece Hall	8%	50
4	Saquon Barkley	5%	49
5	Jonathan Taylor	-1%	41
6	Jahmyr Gibbs	-1%	32
7	Derrick Henry	-4%	32
8	Kyren Williams	-6%	31
9	Travis Etienne Jr.	-8%	30
10	Joe Mixon	-8%	28
11	Rachaad White	-9%	26
12	De'Von Achane	-11%	25

	RB2 PPR	RPV	$
13	Alvin Kamara	16%	22
14	Josh Jacobs	9%	21
15	James Cook	7%	20
16	Zamir White	5%	20
17	Isiah Pacheco	5%	19
18	Aaron Jones	2%	18
19	Kenneth Walker III	-4%	16
20	Raheem Mostert	-7%	15
21	James Conner	-7%	15
22	Austin Ekeler	-9%	14
23	Brian Robinson Jr.	-9%	14
24	D'Andre Swift	-9%	12

	RB3 PPR	RPV	$
25	Rhamondre Stevenson	24%	12
26	David Montgomery	18%	12
27	Najee Harris	18%	12
28	Jaylen Warren	11%	11
29	Tony Pollard	-5%	11
30	Ezekiel Elliott	-8%	11
31	Nick Chubb	-8%	10
32	Zack Moss	-8%	10
33	Devin Singletary	-10%	9
34	Tyjae Spears	-10%	9
35	Jonathan Brooks	-11%	9
36	Javonte Williams	-12%	8

	Player	RPV
1	Christian McCaffrey	30%
2	Breece Hall	10%
3	Derrick Henry	6%
4	Bijan Robinson	4%
5	Saquon Barkley	-1%
6	Jahmyr Gibbs	-1%
7	Kyren Williams	-3%
8	Jonathan Taylor	-5%
9	Joe Mixon	-5%
10	Travis Etienne Jr.	-7%
11	Rachaad White	-12%
12	Isiah Pacheco	-16%

	Player	RPV
13	De'Von Achane	6%
14	Josh Jacobs	4%
15	Alvin Kamara	4%
16	Zamir White	3%
17	Aaron Jones	2%
18	David Montgomery	2%
19	Kenneth Walker III	1%
20	James Cook	1%
21	James Conner	0%
22	Raheem Mostert	-6%
23	Brian Robinson Jr.	-8%
24	Rhamondre Stevenson	-8%

	Player	RPV
25	Najee Harris	16%
26	D'Andre Swift	16%
27	Ezekiel Elliott	12%
28	Zack Moss	8%
29	Austin Ekeler	1%
30	Gus Edwards	-2%
31	Nick Chubb	-2%
32	Tony Pollard	-6%
33	Devin Singletary	-6%
34	Javonte Williams	-10%
35	Jaylen Warren	-13%
36	Jonathan Brooks	-13%

Get updated RPV Cheat Sheets 10 & 12 tm leagues for one time $5 cost (free updates) PayPal: FantasyBlackBook@gmail.com or Venmo: @FantasyBlackBook And include your email address

Yes, wide receivers are all the rage in fantasy these days. The NFL is a pass-first and pass-often league. Running backs have been devalued in the NFL Draft, and they struggle to attain sizable second contracts in the NFL. All of this might be sadly true, but we still need running backs in fantasy.

The days of teams deploying bell cows regularly are gone. Do some teams still subscribe to this way of running their offense or managing their depth chart? Sure, but it's a slim few. This does separate the few elites at the position from the many. With wide receivers getting pushed up fantasy football draft boards more and more every year, we are in an interesting era where we can mine volume (and possibly plenty of it) from running back situations in the middle rounds.

Will there be running backs that fit the prototypical dead zone back? Yep, but the running back landscape has plenty of candidates that could emerge from the middle rounds of drafts as some of the best picks in fantasy football. Ok, that's enough setup and introduction. Let's get into it. The outlook for over 50 backs in fantasy football for the 2024 season.

Elite

1. **Christian McCaffrey, SF:** Last year, McCaffrey turned in yet ANOTHER difference-maker season in fantasy football. He was the highest-rostered player on teams that made the fantasy playoffs (72.8%). He was the RB1 in fantasy, finishing as an RB1 in 81% of his games and as a top 24 RB in every game he played. McCaffrey was second in carries, fourth in targets, and first in red zone touches among running backs. There's no reason to expect a falloff entering 2024. He'll be the 1.01 in almost every draft this year yet again.

2. **Breece Hall, NYJ:** Well, so much for a "down season" coming off an injury. Hall dispelled any of those notions last season. He finished the season as the RB6 in fantasy points per game and the RB9 in expected fantasy points per game. In Weeks 5-18, he averaged 20.2 touches and 102.5 total yards. A huge part of his value last season came from his pass game usage, as he led all running backs in targets, receiving yards, and receptions. While some of this was part of the fallout of Zach Wilson at the helm, Hall should remain a focal point for the passing attack in 2024. Hall is a top-five fantasy running back in all formats.

3. **Bijan Robinson, ATL:** Let's all rejoice. Pop the streamers. Run naked through the streets. Arthur Smith is out of Atlanta, which means Bijan Robinson should be unleashed in 2024. Last year, he ranked ninth in snap share, third in targets, sixth in receptions, and fourth in receiving yards among running backs, but he finished as the RB17 in fantasy points per game. Robinson was the RB12 in expected fantasy points per game, but his opportunity share ranked 31st, and he was also 32nd in red zone touches with Smith's insistence on utilizing Tyler Allgeier. Robinson was efficient with his opportunities last season, ranking 11th in yards per touch and 10th in yards created per touch. If Atlanta feeds this beast in 2024, Robinson could challenge McCaffrey for RB1 overall.

Top Target

1. **Saquon Barkley, PHI:** Let's get this out of the way immediately. No, I'm not that worried about Jalen Hurts capping Saquon Barkley's ceiling. Barkley will be the do-it-all three-down workhorse for Philly. Barkley and D'Andre Swift are not close to being in the same talent area code. Bringing in Barkley means we likely see a downtick of Hurts' goalline dives in 2024. While the overall counting stats for Barkley look depressed, he's still very much a bell-cow with plenty left in the tank. Last season, he ranked second in opportunity share and ninth in weighted opportunities while still operating as an explosive player, ranking 15th in breakaway run rate and eighth in breakaway runs. Barkley remains a top-shelf RB1.

2. **Jonathan Taylor, IND:** Taylor had a tumultuous season in 2023, filled with injuries and contract squabbles. We rarely got to witness the player we have loved since he set foot in the NFL but trust me, he's still there and primed for a huge 2024 campaign. In Weeks 7-18, he handled 21 touches per game, churning out 99.4 total yards per game. Despite ranking 25th in yards per touch and 28th in juke rate last year, he's still one of the best pure rushers in the NFL. With Anthony Richardson increasing the efficiency of this ground game, Taylor should be a locked-in RB1 for 2024.

3. **Jahmyr Gibbs, DET:** After the fantasy industry collectively freaked out in the early portions of last season, when it was all said and done, Gibbs paid off on the offseason hype. Gibbs finished the season as the RB8 in fantasy points per game and fantasy points per opportunity. He was a big play waiting to happen, ranking 13th in evaded tackles, eighth in yards per touch, and second in breakaway run rate. After David Montgomery returned from injury, Gibbs averaged 14.1 touches and 73.1 total yards per game. While Montgomery will remain a thorn in Gibbs' side in 2024, that doesn't mean he can't repeat as an RB1 again this year.

4. **Derrick Henry, BAL:** At this point, we need to quit doubting Henry. Year after year, he has buried his doubters under a mountain of broken tackles. Last year was no different, as Henry was ninth in evaded tackles and 24th in juke rate. While he will cross the dreaded age 30 threshold this year, it's tough to project a drop-off for Henry and any reasons that he can't continue to chug along as an RB1., especially when he'll be given plenty of opportunities to spike touchdowns in a run-first offense in 2024. Last year, Baltimore ranked fifth in red zone rushing attempts per game. The king isn't vacating his throne yet. Continue to invest in Henry for 2024.

5. **Travis Etienne, JAC:** From a macro perspective, Etienne appears to have smashed last year as the RB7 in fantasy points per game, but when you look closer, his season was a tale of two halves. In Weeks 1-8, he averaged 22.3 touches and 106.2 total yards as the RB4 in fantasy points per game. After Week 9, his production dropped off a table as he averaged 16.3 touches and 70.5 total yards for the rest of the season as the RB22 in fantasy points per game. Etienne remains an RB1 in 2024, but he's not quite as safe a pick as he might seem.

6. **Joe Mixon, HOU:** Mixon looks primed to gobble up volume in Houston with another RB1 season in 2024. Last year, he was the RB11, ranking eighth in snap share and seventh in weighted opportunities. He could eclipse both of those marks this season. With only Dameon Pierce, Dare Ogunbowale, Jawhar Jordan, and J.J. Taylor behind Mixon, he should be the unquestioned bell cow. Efficiency probably won't be a hallmark of Mixon's game in 2024 after he was 24th in fantasy points per opportunity and 35th in yards created per touch, but as we always say, "volume is king," and Mixon is sure to see a ton of it.

7. **Kyren Williams, LAR:** Last year, Williams made quick work of Cam Akers, and he's likely to do the same with Blake Corum this season. In 2023, Williams was the RB2 in fantasy points per game, first in snap share, and fourth in opportunity share. He was also 20th in breakaway runs, eighth in evaded tackles, and 10th in juke rate. In Weeks 2-17, he averaged 22.3 touches and 117.8 total yards playing at least 72% of the snaps in ten of 11 games played. Corum could steal touches here or there, with most of his dirty work probably coming when the Rams are salting away the clock, but Williams should still be considered the lead back in this offense and an RB1.

8. **De'Von Achane, MIA:** Achane exploded onto the NFL scene last year as the RB4 in fantasy points per game. In the eight games he played at least 41% of the snaps, Achane averaged 14.2 touches and 113.8 total yards. Achane was near the top in every efficiency category, ranking first in yards per touch, third in juke rate, first in breakaway run rate, and first in fantasy points per opportunity. If he can displace Mostert as the leader of this backfield and keep Jaylen Wright at bay, Achane could be a top-three fantasy back this season.

9. **Rachaad White, TB:** Rachaad White was the South Florida version of Joe Mixon last year. He gobbled up snaps and volume while underwhelming in efficiency metrics. Last year, White was the RB10 in fantasy, ranking fourth in snap share, seventh in opportunity share, and fourth in weighted opportunities. He also ranked top-ten in carries (second), targets (ninth), and red zone touches (ninth). White didn't necessarily squander the volume he earned, but he also didn't squeeze every ounce of juice out of it either. White was 34th in fantasy points per opportunity, 33rd in yards per touch, and 23rd in yards created per touch. White could have the stranglehold on volume again in 2024, but don't be surprised if Bucky Irving eats in his snaps some.

Solid Options

1. **Isiah Pachecho, KC:** Pacheco was a rock-solid RB2 last season (RB14). With Jerick McKinnon gone, Pacheco has upside for even more in 2024. In the four games he played without McKinnon active, Pacheco averaged 20.2 touches and 100.7 total yards. He was Kansas City's workhorse, as he played at least 70% of the snaps in three of those four games. Pacheco flashed a solid all-around skill set, ranking 20th in yards per route run, 27th in evaded tackles, and 11th in breakaway run rate. Pacheco is a perfect RB2 to draft this year who could sneak into RB1 territory.

2. **Kenneth Walker, SEA:** Walker hasn't been the monstrous RB1 many have hoped for in the NFL, but that doesn't mean he's been bad. He has finished as the RB16 and RB20 in fantasy points per game in his two seasons of work. Last year, Walker persevered through a bruised shoulder, a strained oblique, a chest issue, and a tender calf to average 17.3 touches and 82 total yards (in the games, he played at least 41% of the snaps). Walker flashed his usual rushing excellence, ranking second in juke rate, third in evaded tackles, and 26th in yards created per touch. Zach Charbonnet will remain a looming specter on the depth chart, but this is Walker's backfield.

3. **Zamir White, LVR:** White is set to soak a metric ton of volume this season as the Raiders' lead back. In Weeks 15-18, he averaged 23.3 touches and 114.3 total yards as the RB12 in fantasy points per game. To put those numbers in context further, when White was the starter, his full-season pace would have ended with 395 touches and 1,942 total yards. Yes, I know it was only four games, but these numbers are insane. If White can hold up for a full season, he should easily eclipse 300 touches. On a per-touch basis, he was also strong, ranking 30th in yards created per touch and 16th in breakaway run rate. White is a strong RB2 who could flirt with RB1 production.

4. **James Cook, BUF:** James Cook took flight after Joe Brady was handed the controls for the offense. In Weeks 11-18, Cook was the RB11, averaging 19.6 touches and 104.3 total yards per game. In the same stretch, he was 16th in target share while also ranking fourth in receiving yards per game and second in yards per route run. Cook's red zone usage will remain a worry for 2024, with not only Josh Allen getting in on the goal-line dive action but possibly also Ray Davis. Cook is another RB2 who could be an RB1 this season, but he does have some volatility to his profile. The risk in many drafts will be properly baked into his ADP.

5. **Alvin Kamara, NO:** Kamara remained the Saints' go-to guy last season. Yes, Kendre Miller's spotty injury issues helped that case, but it was still the truth. Last year, Kamara was tenth in opportunity share, eighth in weighted opportunities, and ninth in red zone touches. Kamara's early down skills have seemingly eroded (46th in juke rate), but his receiving chops are still stout. Last year, he was fourth in yards per route run and second in target share among backs. Kamara might not still be in his prime, but he can still be an RB1/2 for 2024.

6. **Devin Singletary, NYG:** Devin Singletary should be the Giants' volume eater in 2024. Last year in Houston, he proved yet again that he can be a dependable starter. In Weeks 9-18, he averaged 19 touches and 86.6 total yards as the RB21 in fantasy points per game. Singletary was his usual surprising self in the efficiency department, ranking 25th in evaded tackles and 15th in breakaway runs. Singletary's picture resides next to the term "volume-based RB2" in the dictionary.

7. **D'Andre Swift, CHI:** Swift is now the de facto lead back in Chicago after the wallet-stuffing contract he signed with the Bears. As the Eagles' starter last year, Swift finished as the RB24 in fantasy points per game. He should be considered a low-end RB2 again this season. Swift should rip off some big plays again this year after ranking 11th in breakaway runs last year. The big question for him is consistency. In his first four games as the starter for Philly, he averaged 22.3 touches and 126.6 total yards. After that point, he faded badly, averaging only 16.1 touches and 78.5 total yards. With the talented Khalil Herbert nipping at his heels all year, Swift will have to stay at the top of his game to hold him off.

8. **David Montgomery, DET:** Montgomery closed the first chapter of his story as a Detroit Lion convincingly as RB15 in fantasy. Montgomery won't be leaned on as heavily this season as he was to begin last year. We already saw a reduction in his workload after his return from injury last season, when he averaged 15 touches and 75.7 total yards. Montgomery will split work with Jahmyr Gibbs all year, but he's locked in as the early down hammer in one of the league's best offenses. The volume and touchdown opportunities will be there. Last year, he was 15th in carries, fifth in red-zone touches, and fourth in rushing touchdowns (13). Montgomery, at his floor, is a strong RB3/flex, but he's better viewed as a low-end RB2.

Red Flags

1. **Aaron Jones, MIN:** Aaron Jones is trying to keep Father Time at arm's length for at least one more year. I won't bet against him being able to do so, but there's some risk with selecting him in fantasy football. Jones struggled with injuries for most of last season, but when he finally was healthy, he performed like the stud lead back we have loved for years. In Weeks 15-20, Jones averaged 21.6 touches and 120.3 total yards as he was a weekly stud. During that same stretch, he was 10th in yards after contact per attempt. Jones is an RB2 who still has RB1 upside if his health complies.

2. **Josh Jacobs, GB:** All the volume that Josh Jacobs absorbed in 2022 took its toll on him in 2023. He was only able to play 13 games while missing the back half of the season with a quad strain. Jacobs looked like a shadow of his former self last year. He ranked 53rd in juke rate and 31st in evaded tackles while mustering only five breakaway runs all season. Jacobs should be the 1A in the Green Bay backfield, but I'm not sure he will live up to any lofty notions anyone has of him reclaiming his 2022 glory. Talented rookie MarShawn Lloyd will push Jacobs for volume for the entire season. Jacobs could return value as a volume-based RB2 in Green Bay's high-scoring offense.

3. **James Conner, ARI:** James Conner is coming off arguably his best season as a pro. He rushed for a career-high 1,040 rushing yards while finishing as the RB13 in fantasy points per game. His per-touch metrics were all wonderful, as he ranked 16th in yards per touch and yards created per touch while also sitting at 10th in evaded tackles. Conner will lead the way for Arizona again in 2024, but now he will have Trey Benson to deal with. We could see Arizona split up the volume more evenly this year in an attempt to keep Conner healthy. Conner is a low-end RB2/3.

4. **Brian Robinson, WAS:** Robinson doesn't get nearly enough credit for how good he was last year. In the 12 games in which he played at least 40% of the snaps, Robinson averaged 15.5 touches and 77.9 total yards per game. Robinson was the RB14 in fantasy points per opportunity and the RB22 in fantasy points per game. He was also strong in efficiency and tackle-breaking metrics, ranking 20th in evaded tackles and seventh in yards created per touch. Don't sleep on his pass game upside despite Austin Ekeler's arrival, as Robinson was fifth in yards per route run last season. Robinson can be widely drafted as an RB3, but don't be shocked when he's a weekly solid RB2 in 2024.

5. **Rhamondre Stevenson, NE:** Stevenson was a massive disappointment last season. He was coming off an RB10 season in fantasy, but last year, he couldn't come close to matching those numbers. Stevenson finished as the RB27, averaging 71.4 yards. There's hope for a bounceback in 2024, though. In his final four games of the season before being shelved due to injury, he resembled the stud we thought we were drafting. During that stretch, he ranked 13th in missed tackles forced per attempt while averaging 20.7 touches and 112.7 total yards in the games in which he played at least 63% of the snaps. If he builds upon that late-season surge in 2024, Stevenson could be a fantastic value.

6. **Raheem Mostert, MIA:** Let's see if Mostert can defy age and injuries again in 2024. He did so fantastically last year as the RB4 in fantasy while spiking 21 total touchdowns. The Miami offense is a wonderful breeding ground for touchdowns and explosive plays yearly. Mostert could be leading the way again this season, and while there's risk associated here, in many drafts, it will be included in his ADP. After he finished 17th in yards per touch, seventh in juke rate, and 10th in evaded tackles last year, there's hope he has at least one more stellar season left in him. If he can keep De'Vone Achane and Jaylen Wright at arm's length, Mostert could be an RB2 with upside for more.

7. **Tony Pollard, TEN:** Ok, let's get this out of the way. Tony Pollard was one of my biggest misses last year. I didn't see one of the most explosive backs in the NFL losing his Superman abilities and operating as Clark Kent for most of the year. Despite Pollard falling (WAY) short of my lofty expectations in 2023, he did get the role for Dallas that we all hoped for. He was seventh in snap share, 13th in opportunity share and second in red zone touches. The problem again was he didn't capitalize on the workload. Pollard was the RB11 in expected fantasy points per game and the RB23 in fantasy points per game. He was 44th in yards per touch and 37th in yards created per touch. I will say his numbers did improve after Week 10, as he ranked 15th in yards after contact per attempt for the remainder of the season. If he can give us more consistent flashes of the player we had come to love, he could be an RB2 in 2024. Tyjae Spears will push him all season, so Pollard had better start fast, or this could become a frustrating committee.

8. **Zack Moss, CIN:** This offseason, Moss capitalized on his fortuitous run as the Colts' starter in 2023. After signing as a free agent with Cincy, he should be the Bengals' starter in 2024. Yes, Chase Brown will be involved, but Moss should see the bulk of the work. Last year, in the seven games he started, he played at least 50% of the snaps, and he finished with 21.1 touches and 98.5 total yards per game. Moss ranked 29th in yards per touch and 27th in breakaway runs. Even if Brown caps his passing game upside, Moss should be the goal line back in one of the league's best offenses, which puts him on the RB2/3 radar.

9. **Najee Harris, PIT:** Drafting Harris this season won't leave you pumping your fists, but that doesn't mean he isn't a solid player to target. Last year, his stock dipped as he finished as the RB30 in fantasy points per game, but he still finished with 284 touches, over 1,200 yards, and eight total touchdowns. Jaylen Warren will still be involved weekly, so that caps Harris' upside, but he should still be projected as an RB3 with RB2 upside if the touchdowns lean in his direction. The narrative around Harris has been that he is not an explosive player, but the numbers last season don't line up with that. Harris ranked 12th in evaded tackles, 10th in breakaway run rate, and fourth in breakaway runs. Pittsburgh invested heavily in their offensive line this offseason. With those personnel decisions and the arrival of Arthur Smith, I expect them to run the ball down opponents' throats all season. Harris doesn't profile as a league-winning selection in drafts, but that doesn't mean you should be avoiding him.

10. **Javonte Williams, DEN:** Unfortunately, last season, Williams looked every bit like a player who was attempting to rebuild himself and his career after a catastrophic knee injury. Volume wasn't the problem, as he rolled up 264 touches, but his tackle-breaking metrics were an eye-sore. Williams was 55th in fantasy points per opportunity, 53rd in yards per touch, and 36th in yards created per touch. Is it possible he more closely resembles the stud back we were waiting for the massive breakout for in 2024? Yep. It's also equally possible this is just who Wiliams is at this juncture. Williams should be Denver's early down grinder this year, but Sean Payton has already alluded to the fact that the best players will play. Williams feels like a risky RB2/3.

11. **Nick Chubb, CLE:** Nick Chubb is a tough player to draft in 2024 with any semblance of confidence. Yes, that could change as we move through the offseason, but at the time of writing, his outlook is murky at best. His 2023 season was abruptly ended, thanks to a horrible injury. I won't fully doubt any player as they attempt to return from injury, but if we're being honest, the deck is stacked against him. Chubb will be entering his age-29 season, and it's difficult to consider him anything more than a dart throw RB3.

Up and Coming

1. **Jaylen Warren, PIT:** Warren remains one of the best running backs in the NFL, and while that might sound hyperbolic to some, let's look at his numbers from last year. Warren ranked inside the top ten among backs in yards per touch, evaded tackles, juke rate, yards per route run, and every breakaway metric. Warren was an RB2 or better in weekly scoring in 50% of his games. He will again split work this season with Najee Harris, which could cap his upside if Harris stays healthy. If Harris were to miss any time, Warren would be an immediate RB1, but with Harris factored in, Warren is an RB3 who could sneak into the top 24 in the position (RB29 last season).

2. **Jerome Ford, CLE:** The uncertainty swirling around the Browns' backfield could make him a screaming value this year. Nick Chubb is not a sure thing for 2024. D'Onta Foreman and Nyheim Hines are limited journeyman types who will have defined backup roles. Ford is the only back they have that could play every down. Last season, in Weeks 3-17, when Ford was the starter, he averaged 14.9 touches and 66.6 total yards as the RB20 in fantasy. On a per-touch basis, Ford was also fantastic, ranking 19th in yards per route run, 25th in evaded tackles, and 22nd in breakaway runs. If Chubb is an afterthought this season, Ford could be a plug-and-play RB2 again in 2024.

3. **Jaleel McLaughlin, DEN:** McLaughlin has been a love list player for me all offseason. I won't apologize for being enamored with efficient players who also aren't expensive in fantasy football drafts. McLaughlin had a strong rookie season that could springboard into a full-time role in the Denver offense in 2024 as Sean Payton's "Joker." Regardless of whatever efficiency metric you are in love with, McLaughlin pops as he was ninth in fantasy points per opportunity, 10th in yards per touch, sixth in yards created per touch, and 13th in breakaway run rate. Javonte Williams and Audric Estime will fight for the early down role, while Samaje Perine could be cut by the time you read this. McLaughlin is the favorite for passing downs, although he will still have to win the job over Blake Watson. If McLaughlin earns Sean Payton's trust, he could be an RB3/4 that vaults into steady RB2 production (especially in PPR formats).

4. **Jonathon Brooks, CAR:** At the time of penning this, Brooks is still recovering from a torn ACL. Once he is deemed ready to go, he could take over the Carolina backfield quickly. The Panthers spend second-round NFL Draft capital to secure his services, and with only replacement-level talents in Chuba Hubbard and Miles Sanders, Brooks could be the guy late in the 2024 season. However, Hubbard and Sanders will likely help him shoulder the load to begin the season. Brooks displayed a three-down skillset last year at Texas, ranking 21st in yards after contact per attempt and yards per route run while also finishing ninth in PFF elusive rating. Brooks should begin the season as an RB3/flex with the opportunity to be a stretch run hammer that never leaves your fantasy lineup.

5. **Tyjae Spears, TEN:** Tony Pollard's signing crushed our dreams of Spears as a clear RB1 candidate this year, but that doesn't mean he is useless in fantasy. Spears could be 2021 Tony Pollard to Tony Pollard this season. He proved more than capable of operating as a big play compliment to a lead back last year. Spears was the RB38 in fantasy points per game despite only logging three total touchdowns. He finished the year with 152 touches and 838 total yards, which are marks he could easily eclipse in 2024. Spears was 11th in yards per route run, fifth in breakaway run rate, and 23rd in evaded tackles last year. If Tennessee's offense surprises this year, Spears could be Jaylen Warren 2.0.

6. **MarShawn Lloyd, GB:** During the NFL Draft cycle, MarShawn Llloyd was one of my ultimate man crushes. I have never viewed his landing in Green Bay as a bad thing. Will Josh Jacobs be involved? Yep. Is that a coffin nail for Lloyd? Nope. Green Bay has utilized multiple backs during Matt LaFleur's tenure. If Jacobs looks like the player we saw last year in Vegas and not his 2022 self, Lloyd will play an even bigger role in this backfield than even I'm projecting. Lloyd has the talent to surpass expectations. In each of his final two seasons in college, he finished in the top 20 in yards after contact per attempt, breakaway percentage, and PFF elusive rating. This is the type of player we should look to roster heavily at his RB3/4 price tag because if Jacobs misses any time or falters, Lloyd will smash.

7. **Trey Benson, ARI:** Benson lands in Arizona and will help manage the workload of James Conner in 2024. Could Benson earn plenty of work as the season rolls along and make this a true 50/50 split? We'll see, but it's definitely possible. Benson's big play ability makes him a viable fantasy asset, even on limited volume. Over the last two collegiate seasons, Benson has ranked 10th and third in breakaway percentage and 42nd and first in elusive rating (per PFF). Arizona was fourth in neutral script rushing rate last season, so there should be rushing volume for Benson to effectively garner 6-10 touches weekly (with upside for more). Benson starts the season as a flex option with priority handcuff status. Conner's health and performance will dictate how much upside we could see this year on top of that.

8. **Rico Dowdle, DAL:** The Dallas Cowboys will likely operate in 2024 with a running back by committee. Now, the head of that committee and how much work he absorbs is still up for debate, but Rico Dowdle has my vote for committee chairperson. Dowdle will spar with Jerry Jones favorite Ezekiel Elliott weekly for the team lead in touches. Last season in limited duty, Dowdle ranked ninth in yards created per touch and 18th in juke rate. Could Dowdle be the next Alexander Mattison? It's possible, but I'm willing to make the bet that he surprises people in 2024. He's an RB3/4 who could easily post RB2 numbers and run away from Elliott with the job.

9. **Kimani Vidal, LAC:** Kimani Vidal should be in the mix for the starting job for Los Angeles. Gus Edwards and J.K. Dobbins aren't exactly impervious competition that can withstand all challengers. Last year, Vidal ranked 21st in PFF's elusive rating while proving he can handle volume with at least 23 carries in 57% of his games. The one thing we can count on Greg Roman for at this point is that his offense will feature a ton of rushing volume. From 2019-2022 with Baltimore, Roman coordinated an offense that ranked first in neutral rushing rate. Vidal could start slowly out the gate, but look for him to assert himself in this backfield by midseason with the opportunity to take over fully.

Matchup Plays

1. **Austin Ekeler, WAS:** Austin Ekeler, like Fantasy GMs, is likely still trying to process the flameout that occurred last season. Yes, the ankle sprain he suffered in Week 1 likely played a part in his "down season," but that can't be the culprit we use to explain away everything we saw last year. Once he returned from injury, he averaged 16.1 touches and 69.2 total yards as the RB28 in fantasy points per game. The fall from fantasy football grace happened so quickly, but that's the same road many aging running backs have walked before him. Ekeler did manage to retain his receiving ability last year, as he ranked eighth in target share and 10th in yards per route run. His rushing skills were the facet that took the biggest hit, as he was 36th in juke rate and 46th in breakaway run rate. Landing in Washington with Anthony Lynn was one of the better-case scenarios this offseason. Ekeler will be an RB3/flex that will likely see elevated usage in games in which Washington trails.

2. **Antonio Gibson, NE:** Gibson signed with the Patriots during the offseason to operate in the "Kareem Hunt role" for New England. New England's new offensive coordinator, Alex Van Pelt, was calling plays for the Browns from 2020-2023. We have seen how his backfields play out. Gibson could siphon off routes from Rhamondre Stevenson immediately while also cutting into his early down and red zone workloads. Gibson proved last year that he can be supremely effective in this role as he was first in missed tackles forced per attempt and eighth in yards after contact per attempt. If Stevenson falters out the gate like he did last season, don't be shocked if Gibson becomes New England's primary ball carrier in 2024. For now, he is best viewed as a flex play that will see more work when the Pats are behind in games.

3. **Gus Edwards, LAC:** Who will be the Bolts' starting running back in 2024? This question could help define the fantasy running back landscape. One of the players in the mix for it could emerge as a wonderous value in fantasy football drafts. Gus Edwards will attempt to put his best foot forward to earn this role with J.K. Dobbins and Kimani Vidal likely his strongest competition. Edwards has a long history with new offensive coordinator Greg Roman. Roman knows exactly what he's likely to get from Edwards. An early down bulldozer that can punch in short scores. Last season, Edwards was the RB32 in fantasy, with the strength of 13 total touchdowns (fourth-most). Edwards looks like a player on the decline in the rushing department after finishing 51st in juke rate, 39th in evaded tackles, and 45th in yards created per touch last season. If Edwards emerges with the job, he's a weekly RB2/3 who likely needs a score to pay off.

Handcuffs to Know

1. **Zach Charbonnet, SEA:** Charbonnet was a complementary role player in his rookie season. He was thrust into the starter's chair for three games when Kenneth Walker was banged up. In the three games that he played at least 61% of the snaps, he averaged 19.7 touches and 75.3 total yards, with two top-18 running back finishes (RB18, RB13). Charbonnet made plays last season when he was given opportunities, ranking 14th in yards created per touch and 21st in breakaway run rate. Charbonnet is a priority handcuff who could step into any fantasy lineup as an RB2 if Walker were to miss time.

2. **Chase Brown, CIN:** How much will Chase Brown impact Zack Moss's workload in 2024? Will he have flex value weekly, or is he just a high-end handcuff? We'll see how all of this shakes out during the season, but for now, he's best seen as a handcuff. Brown was effective last year when called upon, ranking 12th in fantasy points per opportunity with strong numbers in yards per route run and juke rate. Brown could force a messy committee situation in Cincy if he replicates his rookie season playmaking. Get exposure to him in drafts this season.

3. **Blake Corum, LAR:** Corum slots in as the primary handcuff to Kyren Williams immediately, and he could get work on early downs and in a positive game script. The Rams showed how much they liked him by selecting him in the third round of the NFL Draft. I have worries about Corum (probably more than the Rams apparently do). All of his elusiveness metrics and tackle-breaking numbers declined in each of his last three seasons in college. Yes, we can explain some of this away because of injury, but the problem started before Corum dealt with injuries at Michigan. If Williams misses any time this season, Corum would immediately be a top 24 running back play. He's one of the best handcuffs to draft in 2024.

4. **Kendre Miller, NO:** Miller never had a chance to get on track in his rookie season. Injuries followed him with every step. Miller was only able to play in eight games while crossing the 30% snap mark three times. With his limited volume, he did, however, post impressive numbers in tackle-breaking. This is still Alvin Kamara's backfield, so Miller falls into the middling handcuff territory because even if Kamara misses time, Miller is likely to have to fight Jamaal Williams for snaps.

5. **Elijah Mitchell, SF:** Mitchell remains Christian McCaffrey's understudy. Despite his struggles to stay healthy, the handcuff role is still likely Mitchell's to lose. Mitchell played only 11 games last year and logged 81 touches. Jordan Mason and Isaac Guerendo will likely push Mitchell for the RB2 spot on the depth chart. This downgrades him to only a middle-tier handcuff, whereas he was near the top of the heap in previous draft seasons.

6. **Khalil Herbert, CHI:** Khalil Herbert has consistently finished near the top of the list for tackle-breaking metrics over the last few seasons. It saddens me that Chicago felt like they needed to upgrade the position this offseason with the signing of D'Andre Swift. Herbert trounced him in efficiency metrics last season, ranking 21st in juke rate, 19th in yards per touch, and 12th in breakaway run rate. Despite this fact, Herbert is only a handcuff this season but a very good one that could offer RB2 plug-and-play ability if Swift were to be struck with an injury.

7. **Jaylen Wright, MIA:** Wright is a wonderful dice roll this season that could yield outstanding results if things break his way. At the time of writing, he appears firmly third on the rushing depth chart behind Raheem Mostert and De'Von Achane. It only takes one injury or a reshuffling of the deck to change that. Wright is an immensely talented player, and I loved him the entire draft cycle. During his final collegiate season, he ranked fifth in yards after contact per attempt and 13th in PFF's elusive rating. If you're willing to embrace uncertainty, Wright could reward you handsomely this season.

8. **Ezekiel Elliott, DAL:** Zeke is back! After a one-year dalliance with New England, he returned to Jerry Jones' warm embrace. Unfortunately, Elliott looked like a back on his last legs last season. He ranked outside the top 30 backs in evaded tackles, fantasy points per opportunity, and juke rate. He'll work with Rico Dowdle this season. The division of labor in this backfield is up in the air, but I strongly prefer Dowdle in every format. Elliott could offer flex value and, in theory, is the primary handcuff. He's just not a player I'm excited to press the draft button this season.

9. **Evan Hull, IND:** Oh, what could have been last year for Evan Hull? If he hadn't gotten injured in Week 1, it could have been him going ballistic weekly instead of Zack Moss when Jonathan Taylor was sidelined. Unfortunately, it didn't happen, but Hull should enter this season as Taylor's immediate backup. Hull proved in college he has a three-down skillset with over 1,400 total yards and a 17.3% target share in his final season at Northwestern. If Taylor misses any time this season, Hull should eat as the Colts' three-down workhorse.

10. **Tyrone Tracy Jr., NYG:** Tracy should have no issues earning the RB2 job for the Giants. Eric Gray did nothing in his rookie season to have an automatic leg up in the room. Last year, Gray could only manage 2.8 yards per carry and 1.53 yards after contact per attempt (per PFF). Tracy (a converted wide receiver) has underrated receiving upside that Purdue never capitalized on, but that doesn't mean New York won't. In his final collegiate season, Tracy ranked fourth in yards after contact per attempt and fifth in elusive rating (per PFF). Singletary likely hogs all the work if he is healthy all season, but if he misses any time, Tracy would be an immediate weekly RB2.

11. **Ray Davis, BUF:** Davis enters the Bills' depth chart and should be considered the immediate favorite to secure the RB2 spot. Davis can add a little bit of everything to a running back room. He has proven the ability to carry the load in college while also displaying at least serviceable receiving skills. In his final collegiate season, Davis ranked 27th in yards after contact per attempt and 34th in breakaway rate (per PFF). Davis falls into the lower tier of handcuffs, but he could offer standalone flex value immediately.

12. **Chuba Hubbard, CAR:** I easily could have written up Miles Sanders for this section of the Black Book. Yes, Hubbard was the leading back last year, but there's no telling who will be asked to help Brooks carry the load as he gets up to speed. I'll side with Hubbard slightly because of how badly we saw Sanders falter last season, even when he was healthy. Hubbard at least performed well as the starter. In Weeks 6-18, as the RB24 in fantasy points per game, he averaged 19.2 touches and 77.7 total yards. There are better handcuffs with clearer paths to work to target this season.

13. **Dameon Pierce, HOU:** The fall for Dameon Pierce came swiftly, coming off the heels of a stellar rookie season. In Weeks 1-8, he averaged 16.9 touches, producing only 58.7 total yards. He was running behind an offensive line that was beaten up and struggling in those first seven games, so that does have to factor in here to a small degree. However, he still wasn't able to wrestle the job away from Devin Singletary ever after he and the offensive line got healthy in the back half of the season. With Joe Mixon in Houston with a newly signed contract, Pierce's chances of reclaiming the starting job are absolutely zero, but the rest of the running back depth chart behind him is even worse. If Mixon were to go down, Pierce would be the guy to get all the work.

14. **Tyler Allgeier, ATL:** With Arthur Smith jettisoned, Atlanta should lean on Bijan Robinson, but Tyler Allgeier should also be the clear handcuff to Robinson. Allgeier couldn't follow up his standout rookie campaign, as he was only 43rd in yards per touch, 54th in fantasy points per opportunity, and 47th in breakaway runs. He would fall into the low-end handcuff tier with volume-based RB2 if Robinson were sidelined.

15. **Bucky Irving, TB:** Despite flopping in the pre-draft athletic testing (2.22 RAS), Irving still got fourth-round NFL Draft capital. He should be the primary backup to Rachaad White and the clear handcuff if he goes down. Last year, he ranked 17th in yards after contact per attempt and eighth in elusive rating (per PFF). If White reprises his same role from last season, Iriving offers little to no standalone value. He's just a run-of-the-mill handcuff.

16. **Ty Chandler, MIN:** Ty Chandler was a serviceable starter last year when he was called upon, but with Aaron Jones in town now, he's regulated to backup duties. In Weeks 15-18, he played at least 53% of the snaps in every game, averaging 15.3 touches and 81.8 total yards. Chandler's per-touch efficiency was abysmal, so it's not surprising that Minny felt they had to upgrade in the offseason. He ranked 31st in juke rate and 32nd in fantasy points per opportunity. Chandler is another bargain bin handcuff that can be picked up in the later rounds of a fantasy draft or possibly even after the draft concludes on waivers.

Chapter 6

Wide Receiver Profiles

Andrew Erickson

	WR1 PPR	RPV	$
1	CeeDee Lamb	23%	60
2	Tyreek Hill	13%	51
3	Ja'Marr Chase	12%	50
4	Amon-Ra St. Brown	8%	48
5	Justin Jefferson	2%	42
6	A.J. Brown	-1%	37
7	Puka Nacua	-3%	36
8	Garrett Wilson	-8%	31
9	Marvin Harrison Jr.	-8%	30
10	Chris Olave	-9%	28
11	Drake London	-14%	26
12	Nico Collins	-14%	25

	WR2 PPR	RPV	$
13	Davante Adams	8%	25
14	DJ Moore	6%	24
15	Mike Evans	6%	24
16	Michael Pittman Jr.	5%	23
17	Jaylen Waddle	4%	22
18	Cooper Kupp	2%	21
19	Brandon Aiyuk	0%	20
20	Deebo Samuel Sr.	0%	20
21	DK Metcalf	-6%	19
22	Terry McLaurin	-6%	19
23	Amari Cooper	-8%	18
24	Tee Higgins	-8%	18

	WR3 PPR	RPV	$
25	Malik Nabers	4%	17
26	Chris Godwin	4%	17
27	DeVonta Smith	3%	16
28	Stefon Diggs	2%	16
29	Keenan Allen	2%	16
30	Zay Flowers	-1%	15
31	Christian Kirk	-1%	15
32	George Pickens	-1%	15
33	Christian Watson	-1%	15
34	Tank Dell	-3%	13
35	Hollywood Brown	-4%	12
36	DeAndre Hopkins	-5%	11

	WR4 PPR	RPV	$
37	Diontae Johnson	7%	11
38	Ladd McConkey	6%	10
39	Courtland Sutton	6%	10
40	Jordan Addison	5%	10
41	Jayden Reed	3%	9
42	Calvin Ridley	3%	9
43	Tyler Lockett	2%	8
44	Jakobi Meyers	-3%	7
45	Xavier Worthy	-6%	5
46	Jaxon Smith-Njigba	-7%	4
47	Adam Thielen	-7%	4
48	Mike Williams	-9%	3

	WR5 PPR	RPV	$
49	Romeo Doubs	12%	3
50	Brandin Cooks	12%	3
51	Rome Odunze	10%	3
52	Rashid Shaheed	7%	2
53	Brian Thomas Jr.	4%	2
54	Rashee Rice	1%	2
55	Curtis Samuel	-3%	2
56	Jerry Jeudy	-6%	2
57	Keon Coleman	-6%	1
58	DeMario Douglas	-7%	1
59	Jameson Williams	-9%	1
60	Kendrick Bourne	-16%	1

Get updated RPV Cheat Sheets 10 & 12 tm leagues for one time $5 cost (free updates) PayPal: FantasyBlackBook@gmail.com or Venmo: @FantasyBlackBook And include your email address

	WR1 STND	RPV
1	CeeDee Lamb	26%
2	Tyreek Hill	21%
3	Ja'Marr Chase	16%
4	Amon-Ra St. Brown	14%
5	Justin Jefferson	7%
6	Puka Nacua	-8%
7	A.J. Brown	-8%
8	Garrett Wilson	-10%
9	Marvin Harrison Jr.	-13%
10	DJ Moore	-14%
11	Nico Collins	-15%
12	Mike Evans	-15%

	WR2 STND	RPV
13	Davante Adams	9%
14	Drake London	8%
15	Chris Olave	6%
16	Brandon Aiyuk	4%
17	Deebo Samuel Sr.	4%
18	Cooper Kupp	-2%
19	DK Metcalf	-2%
20	Amari Cooper	-4%
21	Jaylen Waddle	-5%
22	Tee Higgins	-5%
23	DeVonta Smith	-5%
24	Stefon Diggs	-7%

	WR3 STND	RPV
25	Michael Pittman Jr.	8%
26	Keenan Allen	6%
27	Terry McLaurin	5%
28	Zay Flowers	4%
29	George Pickens	3%
30	Malik Nabers	2%
31	Christian Watson	2%
32	Chris Godwin	-4%
33	Tank Dell	-4%
34	Christian Kirk	-6%
35	Jayden Reed	-6%
36	Hollywood Brown	-10%

	WR4 STND	RPV
37	DeAndre Hopkins	13%
38	Diontae Johnson	8%
39	Tyler Lockett	6%
40	Courtland Sutton	4%
41	Calvin Ridley	-1%
42	Jordan Addison	-1%
43	Romeo Doubs	-1%
44	Jakobi Meyers	-3%
45	Brandin Cooks	-3%
46	Ladd McConkey	-6%
47	Xavier Worthy	-6%
48	Rashid Shaheed	-10%

	WR5 STND	RPV
49	Gabe Davis	12%
50	Jerry Jeudy	10%
51	Curtis Samuel	9%
52	Adam Thielen	6%
53	Mike Williams	3%
54	Brian Thomas Jr.	0%
55	Rome Odunze	-1%
56	Jaxon Smith-Njigba	-5%
57	Rashee Rice	-7%
58	Jameson Williams	-8%
59	Keon Coleman	-9%
60	Kendrick Bourne	-11%

***Get updated RPV Cheat Sheets 10 & 12 tm leagues for one time $5 cost (free updates) PayPal: FantasyBlackBook@gmail.com or Venmo: @FantasyBlackBook
And include your email address***

The fantasy football landscape has changed at the very top to slightly favor the league's top-tier WRs, such as Justin Jefferson, Ja'Marr Chase, Tyreek Hill and CeeDee Lamb. But this isn't the first time we have seen elite WRs favored against their running back counterparts. It wasn't so long ago that the elite tier of WRs like Julio Jones and Antonio Brown were drafted in the top half of Round 1. So, seeing WRs being drafted ahead of many of the RBs is just part of the natural fantasy football cycle. Right now, there's a strong argument that today's top WRs are just better than the top RBs. I still prefer following the "hero RB" approach, locking in my RB1 slot with one player, and then going aggressively after WRs.

The name of the game with wide receivers remains to scoop up value in the middle-to-later portions of drafts, with the position counting for the biggest part of your roster. Take advantage of WRs that fall in ADP, while other teams "reach" for running backs that they think they need. You will be shocked how quickly the WR position dries up despite the false narrative that the position is deep every year. It's not deep. If anything, it's extremely diluted, which makes it much more essential you draft the remaining wideouts toward the start of the middle rounds. You'll feel (and perform) much better knowing you aren't trudging out WRs ranked outside the top 40 as your weekly WR3. Wide receivers in the middle rounds are often the ones that tend to take massive leaps and vastly outperform their ADP.

And when in doubt, just keep drafting WRs (especially rookies) that have breakout potential. Chances are they all won't hit...but all you need is one to hit big to reap the benefits. And if you can draft a truly elite fantasy WR in Round 1 or 2 as alluded to at the top, it's worth it. Because after the elite guys, we see things stagnate and scoring flatten. Wideouts ranked sixth to 20th fluctuate between 15 and 12.5 PPG. Receivers from 21st to 46th score between 12 and 9.5 PPG. Ergo, non-elite fantasy WRs are basically all just fantasy WR2s. And low-end fantasy WR2s are just a massive tier that leaks into the WR4 range.

Elite

1. **Ja'Marr Chase, CIN:** Ja'Marr Chase finished with an impressive stat line last season with 100 receptions, which was a career-high on 145 targets. Chase owned a 26% target share, amassing over 1,200 yards. Chase scored 7 touchdowns while ranking top-10 in red zone targets. The Bengals offense ranked third in pass rate over expectation in the red zone. Over 16 games, Chase averaged a strong 13.3 points per game as the WR13. But we all know Chase left production on the table without his healthy star QB. From Weeks 1-10 with Joe Burrow, Chase averaged 16.2 points per game as the WR6 and scored 19.6 expected points per game, which ranked 5th. Chase has a strong chance to lead the NFL in red zone targets in 2024. He led the NFL in red-zone targets per game over the last TWO SEASONS. In his last 23 games played with Burrow – Chase has averaged nearly two red-zone targets per game. 43 total and the same rate as CeeDee Lamb this past season...Red-zone targets are the path of least resistance to No. 1 overall WR seasons. The last 5 No. 1 overall WRs...finished first in the NFL in red-zone targets. Chase red-zone targets and draft Chase as the No. 1 WR in fantasy football.

2. **Justin Jefferson, MIN:** Justin Jefferson finished the season 5th in points per game (16.8) despite missing seven games and losing starting quarterback Kirk Cousins. Still, he had a standout season with 68 receptions from 100 targets, gaining a total of 1,074 receiving yards. He commanded a 28% target share, 41% air yards share and ranked 8th in weighted opportunity. Before Cousins' injury, he led all WRs in fantasy points scored (21.7 per game). Jefferson's ability to perform without Cousins last season suggests he can still produce in the Vikings 2024 offense that will have a different QB under center. That ambiguity is going to make him fall in drafts. But Weeks 15-18, Jefferson was still a clear-cut ALPHA without Cousins. 18.4 points per game (WR3), averaging 119 receiving yards per game. Believe that whether it's Sam Darnold or 2024 first-round pick J.J. McCarthy as QB1, this Vikings offensive infrastructure set up by Kevin O'Connell will fuel arguably the best WR in the NFL.

3. **CeeDee Lamb, DAL:** Through 18 weeks, CeeDee Lamb finished as the top WR in half-PPR formats, amassing 335 fantasy points at 19.7 per game, which ranked second-best. He had 135 receptions on 181 targets, totaling over 1,700 yards with a long catch of 92 yards. Lamb scored 12 receiving and 2 rushing touchdowns, displaying versatility and consistency throughout the season. Including the postseason,

Lamb posted a 29% target share and flirted with nearly 200 total targets and 2,000 air yards. Ninth in weighted opportunity, No. 2 in fantasy points per snap (0.27) and 19th in air yards share. 1st in red-zone targets, which tends to be the No. 1 predictor of elite WR1 fantasy seasons. Lamb performing so WELL above expectation was tied to his superior roles in the red zone. But the fact that Dallas could never score any rushing TDs despite so many red-zone RBs touches…led to the receivers getting boosted opportunities in the red-zone passing game. Anticipate regression in both facets from pass-to-rush TD/ratio in Dallas for 2024. Dallas had a negative pass rate over expectation in the red zone last season. Over the last 12 seasons, no WR that has led the league in red-zone targets has finished higher than WR3 the following season.

4. **Tyreek Hill, MIA:** Tyreek Hill was second overall in total points among WRs, scoring nearly 300 fantasy points just shy of 20 points per game. No WR had a higher rate of weekly top-6 finishes than the Cheetah (53%). He recorded OVER 1,700 receiving yards from 112 catches on 158 targets, showcasing his deep-threat ability with the longest reception of 78 yards and 12 touchdowns. Hill just turned 30 years old after his best season to date in points per game after averaging a ludicrous league-leading 3.72 yards per route run. He is truly an efficient monster, given he only averaged 67% of the offensive snaps played. There's no wasted effort with Hill in Mike McDaniel's offense. No. 1 WR in fantasy points per snap (0.37).

5. **Amon-Ra St. Brown, DET:** During the fantasy football regular season, Amon-Ra St. Brown finished third averaging 16.5 points per game. He had 112 receptions for 1,371 yards and 9 touchdowns. In the season's entirety, St. Brown commanded a 30% target share (6th) and 34% air yards share. He finished 4th overall in total receiving EPA and 11th in total weighted opportunity. His impressive performance earned him a lucrative 4-year, $120 million contract extension, making him the highest paid WR in the NFL at the time of signing. With Ben Johnson returning as the offensive coordinator, expect the Sun God to burn bright in 2024 and beyond. Only Hill and Jefferson posted higher top-12 weekly finishes last year than St. Brown (47%).

Top Target

1. **A.J. Brown, PHI:** A.J. Brown rounded out the top five WRs, averaging 14.8 per game in 2023. He had 105 receptions for over 1,400 yards and 7 touchdowns, demonstrating his ability to make big plays. Through 10 weeks, only Hill was scoring more fantasy points among WRs. AJB WR1 szn was on full display, logging six straight games with 125-plus receiving yards. Brown's only blemish was he - like the Eagles' entire offense - did not finish strong. From Weeks 11-17 after the bye week, even with Dallas Goedert out of the lineup for a handful of games, AJB was outscored by DeVonta Smith as the WR25 and WR35 in points per game. If the Eagles' late-season collapse trickles over in 2024, Brown's production might take a hit. Give credit to Philly for looking elsewhere to find help on offense, after they hired new offensive coordinator Kellen Moore after a disappointing one-year stint with the Los Angeles Chargers.

2. **Puka Nacua, LAR:** Puka Nacua is the next alpha in the L.A. Rams passing game. The BYU product caught 9 balls for 181 yards and 2 TDs on 10 targets (29%) with 100 yards coming after the catch in his final game of his rookie season, which capped off a historic rookie campaign that saw him break the receptions and receiving yards records for a first-year player. In his 18 games played, Nacua posted a 29% target share (6th in total targets) and averaged 15.3 points per game (4th among all WRs). First in yards after the catch, 3rd in receiving EPA and 14th in weighted opportunity. It should be noted that Nacua's production did dip slightly in games played with Cooper Kupp healthy, who was in the lineup. His fantasy points per game dropped to 12.9 (16th) as he had just 3 TDs in those 11 contests. Each Rams WR averaged over 5 catches per game when playing alongside each other as no team threw more to WRs (72%) than the Rams did in 2023. Nacua had fewer red-zone targets despite playing five more games than Kupp.

3. **Garrett Wilson, NYJ:** Garrett Wilson's 2023 peripheral metrics are tantalizing, with his actual production lackluster based on the horrible QB play in New York this past season. He finished with 95 receptions from a whopping 168 targets, amassing 1,042 receiving yards. Wilson only found the end zone three times. He wrapped up the year with 165.7 fantasy points in half-PPR formats, which placed him 31st overall among wide receivers, averaging 9.7 points per game which ranked 39th. Wilson was targeted on 30% of the Jets' passing plays, the 5th highest share in the league, and he led the NFL with a 46% air yards share. Wilson also finished 5th in snaps played at 92%. Assuming the Jets' quarterback play stabilizes and improves with Aaron Rodgers back at QB, Wilson's ceiling should and will rise even further in 2024. Only the Falcons targeted WRs at a lower rate than the Jets did in 2023. Expect the Jets third year WR to cash in on some serious positive TD regression in 2024.

4. **Brandon Aiyuk, SF:** Brandon Aiyuk operated as the more traditional WR1 in the 49ers offense in 2023, leading the team with nearly 1,500 receiving yards and 8 TDs in 19 games played despite a mediocre role in the red zone. Only 9 red-zone targets. He led the 49ers offense with a 24% target share and 39% air yards share (15th). Finished 20th overall in weighted opportunity. Aiyuk averaged 12.4 fantasy points per game as the WR19 finishing with career-highs across the board in his fourth season. Entering a contract year at age 26, we still may not have seen the best to come from Aiyuk fresh off a second consecutive top-15 WR finish in half-PPR. His efficiency numbers are off the charts as a top-5 finisher in yards per route run in 2023. And he was low-key super consistent, despite all the mouths to feed in the 49ers offense. 67% top-24 finisher rate ranked 4th among all WRs. There's additional room for upside should the team move on from Deebo Samuel who has been rumored to be on the trade block.

5. **Michael Pittman Jr., IND:** Michael Pittman Jr. proved his alpha status all year long in the Colts offense with 109 receptions (7th) on 156 targets, accumulating over 1,100 yards. Like his teammate Josh Downs, he had bad TD production with only 4 TDs. Even so, in 16 games, he racked up nearly 200 fantasy points (WR15 overall), which averages out to 12.2 points per game (WR19). Pittman commanded nearly 1300 air yards (33% air yards share), with a 30% target share to boot - 4th-highest among all WRs. Pittman comes with a super-high floor that could be further unlocked with better TD variance in 2024 should Anthony Richardson take this offense a step further in Year 2. Pittman Jr. had the red-zone targets (finished inside the top-10 and twice the amount of any Colts WR), but just didn't get the red-zone TDs to fall his way. Case in point, Pittman Jr.'s top-24 rate ranked ninth among WRs last season, but he only had two top-12 finishes based on the lack of TDs. He also had only one "bust" game. The addition of second-rounder, Adonai Mitchell, in the draft could enhance the overall offensive output without significantly impacting Pittman's high-end target share. Note that the Colts WRs rarely ever leave the field. Pittman finished 3rd in WR snaps (92%) trailing only DeVonta Smith (96%) and teammate Alec Pierce (95%).

6. **Davante Adams, LV:** Davante Adams showed no signs of slowing down despite the QB carousel in Las Vegas. The alpha WR posted a 45% air yard share with nearly 1,900 air yards, a mark that ranked second among all WRs. Also commanded a league-leading 33% target share with 103 catches on a whopping 175 targets. Adams' ability to find the end zone was on full display as he secured 8 touchdowns, with the second-most red-zone targets in the NFL (29). Adams averaged 12.6 points per game, which placed him as the 18th wide receiver in points per game and WR11 overall. Adams doesn't leave the field – third-highest snap rate among WRs in 2023 – and he continues to earn targets at a hyper rate with the league's 4th-highest target rate per snap played. Even at 31 years old, he's shown to still be QB-proof enough to be a high-end fantasy WR2. Because the Raiders current QB room does raise eyebrows about consistency, and Adams did come off his worst year to date in regard to YAC/reception (3.3) since his second season in the NFL.

7. **Chris Olave, NO:** The usage metrics were ALL there for Chris Olave, who commanded a 25% target share and 40% air yards share with over 1,800 air yards which ranked 8th in the NFL. Olave made a significant impact with 87 catches from 138 targets (12th), and he amassed over 1,100 receiving yards (17th). He found the end zone 5 times and ranked 21st among wide receivers in points per game. 10th in targets per snap. Nothing about Olave's talent suggests he should be a fantasy WR2, but that's likely going to be the case with Derek Carr back at QB. However, the duo showed glimpses of improvement in the second half of the season after the bye week as Olave ranked second in catchable target rate (89%) averaging 12.7 points per game (WR16). Weeks 1-11, Olave's catchable target rate ranked 64th at 76%. Adding Klint Kubiak from the Kyle Shanahan coaching scheme as the Saints new OC also bodes well for Olave to take another step in Year 3. He has severely lacked a high weekly ceiling. Just two top-12 finishes per season two years into the league.

8. **Jaylen Waddle, MIA:** Tyreek Hill will be at the top of nearly every single fantasy football draft, whereas Jaylen Waddle will be drafted much later than in 2024 after his worst professional season to date. WR34 overall and WR24 in points per game. But he still managed over 1,000 receiving yards in 14 games given his top-10 touch per snap rate. The issue was he scored just 4 times. But his 24% target share was still excellent. He also posted his highest yards per route run (6th) and PFF receiving grade of his career (5th). Waddle is a sharp buy-low candidate in a high-powered Miami Dolphins offense.

9. **Drake London, ATL:** Drake London's usage numbers were strong in 2023, commanding a 23% target share and 31% air yards share. Over 1,200 air yards, 69 catches and 905 receiving yards, but with just 2 TDs. The lack of TDs positioned London as the WR39 overall, averaging just 8.7 points per game (WR46). Like many WRs, London's ceiling cannot be realized unless the Falcons improve their QB play. Until that happens, he's a talented real-life WR relegated to fantasy WR3 status. Hello, Kirk Cousins and Michael Penix Jr. to the quarterback rescue. There's no debating that London is an offseason winner, and his rising ADP reflects that in full. The question now becomes, how high is too high to draft London (if at all)? Because chasing the steam of the "highest projected breakout receiver" has not been a profitable one. Two years ago, it was Michael Pittman Jr.. Last year it was Chris Olave. Keep in mind that London has zero top-30 finishes in his first two seasons in the NFL. I know, I know, the QB play is the reason he's been bad. But Garrett Wilson found a way to be a top-26 WR in his first two seasons, with equally as bad, if not worse, QB play. Talented players find a way to produce even in bad spots. Ergo, if London's price becomes too high, just say no. His fantasy outlook needs to be tempered by historical trends suggesting caution with hyped breakout candidates.

10. **Zay Flowers, BAL:** Rookie Zay Flowers emerged as Lamar Jackson's top target in the AFC Championship Game, hauling in 5 of his 8 targets (24% target share) for 115 yards and scoring the Ravens' lone receiving touchdown on a spectacular 54-yard play. As Flowers has done all season, he was the clear-cut No. 1 WR for Baltimore. Flowers led the Ravens in air yards/target share at 24%, totaling over 1,000 air yards, 1,000 receiving yards and 6 receiving TDs (plus one rushing TD) on 86 catches in 18 games. Although his final stat line as the WR29 overall and WR31 in points per game (10.7) suggest he left some production on the table. He finished 11th in route participation among all WRs (88%). Only 3 WRs with route participation that high finished with fewer than 11 points per game. Still, Flowers production was boosted heavily in the absence of Mark Andrews. Without Andrews for 7 games (Week 1 and Week 11 onward) Flowers averaged 13.2 points per game (14th). Weeks 2-10, Flowers averaged 8.2 points per game and only scored 1 TD. Although Flowers' target share only decreased from 24% to 22%. Bodes well for him to remain a focal point of the Ravens passing game with Andrews back in the lineup, but it is very possible he is still the 1B to Andrews' 1A.

11. **Nico Collins, HOU:** Nico Collins' third-year breakout was truly remarkable. The former Michigan product had glimpses of potential in his first two seasons but being paired with rookie C.J. Stroud unlocked his fantasy ceiling. He was a Y-A-C God. Collins totaled nearly 1500 receiving yards with just 1,370 air yards. 641 of his yards came after the catch. He also posted a 24% target share. His 3.11 yards per route run ranked second among all WRs. Only three other players have accomplished this feat since 2017 - Tyreek Hill, Cooper Kupp and Julio Jones. Collins averaged 14.6 points per game in 17 games played and 15.7 points per game in 15 games played alongside Stroud. The one thing fantasy drafters need to be wary of is how much above expectation Collins performed. Only Deebo Samuel scored more points above expectation than Collins did in 2023 in true Kyle Shanahan WR-fashion. There will be some regression in the form of some of his big plays not carrying over yearly. Collins was "only" the WR21 in expected fantasy points per game. And with the arrival of Stefon Diggs, some might be afraid to invest in Collins. However, despite the arrival of Diggs impacting his target share, Collins' efficiency should remain high with another threat on the field to divert defensive attention. The fourth year WR finished third in fantasy points per snap in 2023 trailing only Lamb/Hill. He's got an extremely high ceiling with his consensus projection as the WR10 in half-PPR scoring.

Solid Options

1. **Amari Cooper, CLE:** Amari Cooper's season-long statistics were impressive during the fantasy football season despite playing with 4 different QBs. Cooper finished 10th in yards (1,250) and tied for second behind only Tyreek Hill in 20 yards gains (42). 10th-highest air yards share at 41%. He was 17th in points per game as the WR18 overall through 17 games. And who could forget his EXPLOSION in the fantasy football playoffs with a 51-point burger on the Texans. But projecting Cooper ahead, we can look at his 5-game splits with Deshaun Watson as his QB. His 23% target share and 42% air yards share were in-line with his full season long usage numbers. Averaged just under 100 receiving yards per game. 14.8 fantasy points per game ranked 6th and 15.7 expected fantasy points per game (15th). Even with Jerry Jeudy's addition, Cooper remains the WR1 for the Browns. But be aware that Cooper's not without his warts. He is the king of boom-or-bust given his 40% bust rate in 2023. The ups and downs come out as a wash in season-long numbers, but Cooper's fantasy ride tends to always be a bit bumpy.

2. **Mike Evans, TB:** Mike Evans had a standout season in 2023, finishing as the WR4 overall while averaging 14.4 points per game as the WR8. Despite being 30 years old, Evans showed no decline in performance and remained a top target in the Buccaneers' offense. He recorded impressive numbers with 76 receptions for over 1,200 yards and 13 touchdowns. He saw over 2,200 air yards (No. 1 among all players) through the season's entirety commanding a 25% target share and a whopping 41% air yards share (8th). Evans boomed at a constant clip throughout the season, posting the 4th-highest top-6 finisher rate, 7th-highest WR1 rate, 6th-highest WR2 rate and 8th-highest WR3 rate in half-PPR. The big-bodied WR finished top-10 in points per snap. With him returning to the Buccaneers in 2024, there's little evidence to suggest he won't remain Baker Mayfield's No. 1 target. Especially with his best yards after catch per reception performance recorded in 2023. Although it should be noted that it is a new offense in Tampa Bay with Dave Canales leaving for the Carolina Panthers. Evans will turn 31 in August.

3. **DJ Moore, CHI:** D.J. Moore finished with 96 receptions on 136 targets, accumulating 1,364 receiving yards, and 8 touchdowns in his debut season with the Chicago Bears. These impressive numbers placed him as the 6th overall wide receiver in total fantasy points and 10th in fantasy points per game with an average of 14.0. More impressively, he captured a 43% air yards share within his team, the 4th highest in the league, and garnered a top-10 target share at 29%. His 6th place in weighted opportunity highlighted his key role in Luke Getsy's scheme, combining targets and air yards to showcase his integral role in the Bears' passing game. A notable aspect of Moore's season was his performance with quarterback Justin Fields over 12 games. During this stretch, Moore averaged 16.8 points per game, demonstrating high-end WR1 production. He amassed over 1,100 yards and 8 touchdowns, with an impressive 91 receiving yards per game. Therefore, fantasy managers need to adjust expectations with Fields replaced by rookie Caleb Williams, that will likely hinder Moore's fantasy upside in 2024. As will the addition of a target machine,

WR Keenan Allen and the 9th overall pick in this year's draft, Rome Odunze. Moore likely won't see the same type of target volume he saw in 2023 due to the target squeeze from the other high-caliber WRs. However, his strong efficiency marks will likely sustain based on the favorable looks he should get from opposing defenses given all the other weapons on the Bears offense and his own proven track record of efficient play.

4. **DK Metcalf, SEA:** In 2023, D.K. Metcalf maintained his role as a reliable target for the Seahawks, finishing as the WR16 overall and 20th in points per game with notable contributions. He secured 66 receptions with a 23% target share, accumulating over 1,100 yards and boasting a 40% air yards share (14th). With 37 receptions of 20+ yards (tenth) and 8 touchdowns (fifth-most end-zone targets), he demonstrated his big-play ability and scoring prowess. Despite missing his first game, Metcalf remained a consistent high-end fantasy WR2, potentially benefiting from a heavier pass philosophy under new Seahawks OC Ryan Grubb, known for leading college football in passing yards per game with the Washington Huskies. Metcalf posted the NFL's third highest WR3 finisher rate (87%) trailing only Amon-Ra St. Brown and CeeDee Lamb.

5. **George Pickens, PIT:** In four games with Mason Rudolph, George Pickens averaged a 24% target share, 44% air yards share, 14.6 fantasy points (backend fantasy WR1 numbers) and nearly 100 receiving yards per game. On the year, Pickens hauled in 63 receptions from 106 targets, accumulating 1,140 yards, which translated to a remarkable 18.1 yards per reception Weeks 1-18. Pickens closed out the season with 177.3 fantasy points, which gave him an impressive average of 10.3 points per game, ranking him 33rd among wide receivers in points per game. He finished with a 24% target share (6.5 targets per game) and 41% air yards share (13th in total air yards). Pickens offers more upside if Pittsburgh can find the right guy under center. Both Russell Wilson and Justin Fields offer much more upside than Kenny Pickett, given they are threats to attack downfield (both ranked inside top-8 in deep ball rate in 2023). Pickens will also be a true alpha in 2024, with Diontae Johnson traded to the Panthers. During the first 5 weeks of the 2023 season with DJ sidelined, Pickens was the WR13 in fantasy averaging 12.8 points per game (19th) with a 43% air yards share and 24% target share. Averaged nearly 80 receiving yards per game. Yes, Pittsburgh drafted Roman Wilson in Round 3, but Pickens' constant ascension the past two seasons with flashes of top-12 upside suggests he is on the cusp of a true third-year breakout. Just be wary that the run-heavy nature of an Arthur Smith offense could doom Pickens' breakout, so be price sensitive.

6. **Christian Kirk, JAC:** Christian Kirk played a significant role in the Jaguars' passing game in 2023, securing 57 receptions on 85 targets with a 21% target share. He amassed 787 receiving yards and found the end zone 3 times, averaging 13.8 yards per catch. In 12 games, Kirk averaged 11 fantasy points per game, making him a reliable flex option. When healthy alongside Calvin Ridley, Kirk had a higher target share, positioning him as a potential WR1 in the Jaguars' offense with Ridley replaced by Gabe Davis and rookie Brian Thomas Jr. Those two players will be battling for snaps/targets on the perimeter with Kirk operating naturally inside from the slot. Bodes well for him to see plenty of volume in a high-passing offense. Kirk is an integral part of the Jaguars offense, and they felt his loss in the worst way to close out the 2023 season. He missed the last six games of the season, and the Jaguars went 1-5.

7. **Calvin Ridley, TEN:** Calvin Ridley caught 76 passes for over 1,000 yards in his first year back from a lengthy suspension. He totaled nearly 1,800 air yards on a 22.5% target share and 36% air yards share. He scored 8 touchdowns. Elite usage and role in the Jaguars offense. Across 17 games, he averaged 11.3 points per game, making him a boom-or-bust WR2 in fantasy formats. WR17 overall but WR26 in points per game. He was one of just two WRs (Gabe Davis) to post five top-12 finishes along with *six* outside the top-50. However, Ridley led the entire NFL in end zone targets (24). He was the WR10 in expected fantasy points per game. But he never fully took advantage of his elite opportunities to churn out a fantasy WR1 season. There's no doubt that rhetoric around Ridley will be negative heading into 2024 after the human hype piece failed to deliver. But the only reason Ridley "busted" was because he was getting impossible expectations placed on him for a player who hadn't played since 2021. I'd buy the dip, even in his new home in Tennessee. He signed a massive deal with the Titans as a free agent, to be their new WR1

alongside DeAndre Hopkins and Tyler Boyd. Hopkins was a fringe fantasy WR1 in points per game with Will Levis at QB albeit in a run-heavy offense. Ridley's going to continue to have spiked weeks of production in a more pass-heavy centric offense heralded by new head coach Brian Callahan. A concentrated target share between Hopkins/Ridley would be ideal for fantasy purposes.

8. **DeVonta Smith, PHI:** Over the last two seasons, DeVonta Smith has FEASTED when A.J. Brown or Dallas Goedert has missed games. This past year, Smith was WR16 from Weeks 11-18 after DG got hurt. Including the postseason, Smith averaged 13.6 points per game (backend fantasy WR1 numbers). But before Week 11, Smith was WR25 overall averaging 10.9 points per game (WR29). Again, Smith's talent is undeniable, but it's clear that for him to be a fantasy WR1, somebody else in the Eagles passing game must take a step back. Overall, Smith finished the year 20th in points per game (12.2) with a 24% target share. He's a super high-floor player that should not be overdraft given the injury-dependence on ceiling. Smith finished third WR snaps played and first WR snap rate in 2023 (96%). When you play every single offensive play (or close to it) it's hard to fail when you have Smith's abilities.

Red Flags

1. **Keenan Allen, CHI:** Keenan Allen was a league winner in 2023. Third in points per game. WR8 overall. 3rd in target share at 31%. Yet, he showed no signs of slowing down with Justin Herbert as his QB. But the 32-year-old will face new challenges in 2024, after being traded to the Chicago Bears for a 4th-round pick. Allen himself is hurt by the transaction, given the massive downgrade with rookie QB play, while he battles father time past age 30. Allen has avoided the age cliff up to this point, but a brand-new situation with Caleb Williams could be the beginning of his downfall. Rome Odunze and D.J. Moore will be stiff target competition, and commanding targets at an elite level has been exactly how Allen produced for fantasy the last several seasons. Without double-digit targets every week, Allen will be hard to trust.

2. **Deebo Samuel Sr., SF:** Deebo Samuel was electric during the fantasy football season, finishing as the fantasy WR12 overall in 15 games played averaging 14.2 points per game as the WR9. He ranked second on the team in target share at 22% and second in total TDs with 12 with his dual usage. Samuel finished the year with the most total red zone touches among all WRs. As we project Samuel, two points need to be strongly considered. First, his injury history is based on how physical of a player he is. Second, he may experience impending TD regression given he scored more fantasy points above expectation than any other WR from Weeks 1-17. He was the WR26 in expected points per game. His rushing production is difficult to rely on year-to-year, and Brandon Aiyuk is continuing his ascent into the top-tier WR conversation entering a contract year. Not to mention, Samuel's lack of separation skills showed up at the worst time during the Super Bowl. That lack of production likely influenced the 49ers' selection of 1st-round rookie WR Ricky Pearsall, yet another weapon that could hinder Samuel's production. Not to mention, Samuel has been heavily rumored on the trade block, further clouding his 2024 outlook.

3. **Cooper Kupp, LAR:** Cooper Kupp faced injury challenges throughout the season, impacting his performance, particularly with a career-low yards per route run. Despite maintaining a 26% target share, he finished as WR27 in points per game in 2023 despite TD-boosted production. In the games in which Kupp was healthy alongside Puka Nacua, Kupp averaged 11.9 points per game with 5 receiving TDs. He went over 100 yards four times but was held under 55 receiving yards in his eight other games. At 31 years old in 2024, concerns linger regarding his ability to return to peak form. In addition to poor yards per route run, Kupp posted the worst YAC/reception of his career (5.3). Get out before things get worse for an aging Kupp. He's missed an average of six games over the last two seasons.

4. **Stefon Diggs, HOU:** 2023 was a terrible year for Stefon Diggs. He was WR10 overall, but he averaged just 13 points per game as the WR15 in half-point scoring. And his lackluster finish is what had fantasy football gamers pulling their hair out. From Week 10 onward, Diggs was the WR45 averaging a meager 7.3 points and 42 receiving yards per game. This was right around the time the Bills promoted Joe Brady as their new offensive coordinator after Ken Dorsey was fired following Week 10's loss to the Denver Broncos. And it's not like Diggs wasn't seeing opportunities. On the year, the Bills' polarizing WR finished just below a 30% target share with over 1,800 air yards. 12th overall in weighted opportunity. Even during the bad finish, Diggs still had a 25% target share and strong route participation at 85%. But the major question is was Diggs' lack of production do to his declining skill set? Or an overarching offensive philosophy that removed Diggs as a featured piece of the Bills offense just months before he was sent packing to Houston? Either way it makes it tough to draft Diggs confidently coming off career-lows across the board entering his age 31 season. Even with C.J. Stroud as his QB, competition from both Tank Dell and Nico Collins could mark the end of Diggs' alpha WR status in fantasy football.

5. **Rashee Rice, KC:** Rashee Rice caught 105 balls for 1,200 yards in 20 games played with 8 receiving TDs to go along with a 19% target share during his rookie season. The former standout from SMU averaged 10.9 fantasy points per game, which ranked 29th. His role grew substantially after Week 6, and the rookie delivered, averaging 12.1 points per game - placing him firmly inside the top 20 WRs. Rice finished the year with a 28% target rate per route run - 13th among all WRs last season. He also finished 10th among all WRs in fantasy points per snap. He was Patrick Mahomes's primary underneath option with the lowest average depth of target in the NFL among WRs (5.2). Rice finished the season 6th in targets inside the 10-yard line - more than Travis Kelce. But he has major red flags that cloud his 2024 projection. The Chiefs have completely overhauled their WR room with the additions of veteran Marquise Brown and first-round draft pick, Xavier Worthy. And given Rice's legal situation stemming from high-speed hit-and-run crash earlier this offseason, he will likely be facing a multi-game suspension potentially up to six games, shrouding his availability for the 2024 NFL season.

6. **Tyler Lockett, SEA:** Tyler Lockett is past his prime and he showed it all year long with his very inconsistent play. 43rd in points per game (9.6) and WR33 overall despite a strong 22% target share and over 1,300 air yards. He failed to crack the top 30 WRs for the first time since 2017. It was also the first time he failed to match or exceed D.K. Metcalf in fantasy points scored both cumulatively and in points per game. Lockett recorded 79 receptions on 122 targets, totaling 894 receiving yards. He found the end zone 5 times. Lockett originally looked like a logical cut candidate with him due nearly $28M against the salary cap in 2024 and 2025. But he signed a restructured deal this offseason to stay with Seattle. Regardless, entering his age-32 season, you don't need to squint to see the potential fall for Lockett in fantasy football with Jaxon Smith-Njigba breathing down his neck for opportunity. Lockett is also coming off the worst YAC/reception of his career (2.8).

7. **Quentin Johnston, LAC:** After a disappointing rookie season, Quentin Johnston's fantasy value is on life support. The team moved on from Keenan Allen/Mike Williams, but drafted rookie WR Ladd McConkey 34th overall. The Chargers' new GM has been all sunshine and rainbows regarding the former first-round pick, but the lack of Year 1 production is incredibly concerning. Johnston finished 61st among 63 qualifying WRs in yards per route run (0.88) as a rookie. Josh Palmer caught as many passes (38) as Johnston in 7 fewer games played. Is it too soon to label Quentin Johnston a bust after his rookie season? Nope. The last time we saw QJ on the field, he had 2 receptions for 17 yards in Week 18. He's a bust. Don't be swayed. He played all the snaps (87%) and had all the opportunities/routes with Allen injured the last few weeks of the 2023 season to step up. And he didn't. Journeyman WR Alex Erickson was out-targeting Johnston the last 2 weeks of the season. Proceed with caution.

Up and Coming

1. **Tank Dell, HOU:** As a rookie, Tank Dell posted an identical air yards share to Nico Collins at 31% while falling just short in target share at 21%. The undersized WR posted over 1,000 air yards in just 10 games played. In those games, Dell posted again a 21% target share, 33% air yards share and 14.2 points per game (9th). In the 8 games, Collins and Dell played together - each missed a game with injury - the production was nearly identical. 13.9 points per game for Collins and 14 points per game for Dell. The discounted Texan posted higher rates of top-12 and top-24 finishes (equal in raw finishes). Collins will be drafted AHEAD of Dell in every draft this year. I like the value of taking the rookie breakout LATER come 2024, presuming he is 100% healthy coming off a broken fibula and gunshot flesh wound. C.J. Stoud absolutely loves Dell; he convinced the front office to draft the Houston product back during the 2023 NFL Draft. And more recently, Stroud selected Dell in his 'Perfect Offense' as his slot WR, while opting to leave both Nico Collins and Stefon Diggs off the roster.

2. **Jayden Reed, GB:** Jayden Reed was a dynamite prospect coming out of college, and his rookie campaign further cemented his exciting second-year outlook. Reed didn't always play a full-time role as the Packers' primary slot WR - sub 60% route participation and 56% snap share - but he was always targeted heavily with a 25% target rate per route run and 7th highest-highest touch rate despite a 17% overall target share. He also led all Packers WRs in fantasy points per game at 10.6 - good for WR31 status this past season. He averaged just under 2 yards per route run with ten total touchdowns scored. He finished as a top-12 WR in 33% of his games (12th) and ranked fourth in fantasy points per snap. The concerns with Reed are that his slot role limits his total playing time, and his TDs regress in an offense that loves to spread the wealth. If Christian Watson stays healthy, that will eat into Reed's TD potential along with the other potential touchdown scorers on the Packers' young offense.

3. **Jordan Addison, MIN:** Jordan Addison ended the season with 70 receptions on 108 targets, amassing 911 yards. He was particularly effective in the red zone, scoring 10 touchdowns (5th) on just 17% target share. The Vikings WR totaled over 1,300 air yards. He played in all 17 games, contributing consistently to the Vikings' offense, with a total of 186.3 fantasy points, averaging about 11 points per game (WR28). Addison averaged slightly more points per game 12.2 (22% target share and 4 TDs) versus 10.1 (6 TDs) with Justin Jefferson sidelined. Considering the team will likely be without star tight end T.J. Hockenson to start the 2024 season coming off a torn ACL/MCL (PUP candidate), Addison looks like a strong bet to return early low-end WR2 value in Year 2. However, his fantasy stock will be hurt without Kirk Cousins under center in 2024. Given the downgrade in QB play between Sam Darnold/J.J. McCarthy, it will be difficult for Addison to repeat his double-digit touchdown efforts.

4. **Christian Watson, GB:** Christian Watson's sophomore season was completely derailed by hamstring injuries. He missed the first three weeks of the 2023 season entirely and struggled to put together any consistent production until the final three games of the regular season, when he, unfortunately, pulled his hamstring again. The 6-foot-4 and 208-pound WR scored four TDs, while averaging 17.1 points per game (3rd in the NFL). He averaged 10.6 expected fantasy points per game (28th). He also tallied 13 red-zone targets in just 9 games. Watson also had a whopping 15 end-zone targets during the regular and postseason combined (6th). The 3rd-year WR has a high ceiling when healthy as both a big-play and red-zone threat, but it cannot be realized until he solves his hamstring woes. Offseason reports have been positive regarding Watson's hamstrings, providing some hope that he can put it together in Year 3. Because one cannot forget how elite Watson was as a rookie. His 26% target rate per route run was elite, ranking 17th among all WRs with at least 400 snaps. His 2.47 yards per route run ranked inside the top 10. From Week 10 through Week 18, Watson ranked first in yards per route run (2.78). Over the same span, Watson was the WR9 in both total points and on a per-game basis. In Watson's last 6 games as a rookie (with 80% plus snap share) he averaged 18.7 points per game. He mustered just 9.7 points per game in the last 9 games played in 2023. But over the last 15 games in total, he still averaged 13.3 points per game – same as Ja'Marr Chase from 2023.

5. **Jaxon Smith-Njigba, SEA:** In his first season, JSN managed 63 receptions from 93 targets (17.5% target share), totaling 628 yards and averaging 10 yards per reception. Smith-Njigba only scored 4 touchdowns resulting in 59th in points per game (7.0) as the WR48 overall. But it shouldn't be forgotten that Smith-Njigba suffered a wrist injury that contributed to a slow start during his rookie campaign. He started to hit his stride more from Week 6 onward, where he averaged 8.2 points per game. But still, over this span, his route participation (74%, 50th and 64% snap share) and high-end target competition between Tyler Lockett and DK Metcalf made it tough for JSN to produce. With more opportunities in 2024 at just 22 years old, Smith-Njigba is a cheap and easy breakout candidate if he can overtake one of the other Seattle WRs. He flashed his YAC-ability as a short underneath target, with the 12th-highest YAC/reception (5.9) in 2023. And when he was on the field his targets/snap were nearly identical to his two teammates. There's also a chance we see Seattle throw the ball more than ever with former Washington Huskies coach, Ryan Grubb, hired as Seattle's new OC.

6. **Marvin Mims Jr., DEN:** A low-key winner of the Jerry Jeudy offseason trade was second-year Broncos WR Marvin Mims. Mims' role was redundant with Jeudy's last season, hence his limited playing time. His overall lackluster rookie year was tough due to lack of opportunity. He ran a route on 41% of the dropbacks – a mark that ranked outside the top 100. And that was despite the flashes Mims showed with a 100-yard effort in his second game, along with another 73-yard game when he earned a season-high 5 targets back in Week 3. For his efforts as a return man, Mims was also named Second-Team All-Pro and a Poro Bowler as a returner. Leave the light on for Mims to take off in Year 2 should he start playing a full allotment of snaps, which is much more likely with Jeudy gone. Broncos HC Sean Payton said at the 2024 NFL Scouting Combine, that Mims' progression as a receiver was hindered because he played the same role as Jeudy. WR depth in Denver hurt Mims. Payton also said they were generally happy when they did get Mims involved - duh - and that should continue in Year 2. However, Payton went against his word when he drafted Troy Franklin in the 2024 NFL Draft. He suggested slotting Franklin as the Z, which is the role Jeudy played last season.

7. **Demario Douglas, NE:** Demario Douglas was essentially 2023's version of Jakobi Meyers - a complete afterthought rookie WR that made a Year 1 impact. Although he could not score a TD to save his life. Case in point, his team-leading 561 receiving yards was the most among all players to score 0 TDs in 2023. Therefore, his final WR68 standing does a poor job of projecting him going forward. He was the best playmaker on the Patriots all season. Boasted an 18% target share and finished 4th in YAC/reception among all WRs. Earned 7 targets in his first NFL game. 5-plus targets in his 9 games played, seeing 7-plus in over half those contests. From Week 7 onward, Douglas produced a 21% target share (27th), 25% air yards share, 11 missed tackles and 12.6 expected fantasy points per game (31st). Slightly behind Rashee Rice. Despite his strong showing, the Patriots drafted two WRs in this year's draft inside the top-4 rounds. But make no mistake that "Pop" Douglas is the favorite to be New England's slot man in 2024.

8. **Michael Wilson, ARI:** Michael Wilson's impressive performance in Week 18 showcased his potential in the Arizona Cardinals' passing game. With a 21% target share, he hauled in all 6 of his targets for 95 yards, demonstrating his reliability and big-play ability. Wilson's consistent involvement in the offense, evidenced by running routes on 80% of dropbacks (35th among all WRs), solidifies his role as a full-time contributor moving forward, as long as he can fend off free agent acquisition Zay Jones. His strong finish to the season, averaging 15.5 fantasy points per game in the absence of Marquise Brown, further underscores his value and potential impact in the Cardinals' aerial attack next season. He won't be the No. 1 with Marvin Harrison Jr. and Trey McBride on the roster, but he should still be viewed a clear notch ahead of Jones on the WR depth chart as the No. 2 WR.

Veterans

1. **Chris Godwin, TB:** Unlike Mike Evans, Chris Godwin did not experience the same type of resurgence under Baker Mayfield at QB in 2023. At least when it comes to scoring fantasy points. Godwin led the Buccaneers with 91 catches for 1,1109 receiving yards, but he only caught 3 TDs…in 19 games played. Meanwhile, Evans totaled 14. Godwin's target share (23%) was nearly identical to Evans' (25%). But it was the lack of high-value opportunities that nuked Godwin in fantasy football. As a result, he finished with under 10 fantasy points per game (outside top-36 WRs). No player scored fewer TDs with more receiving yards than Godwin. Based on his usage, he should be closer to a total of double-digit scores versus the 3 TDs he has the past two years. Still, at 28 years old, Godwin could be in for a major bounce back if Evans takes a step back entering his age 31-season. It also works in Godwin's favor that new OC Liam Coen, has suggested this offseason putting Godwin back into the slot in a full-time role. Godwin played his lowest slot snap rate (37%) since 2018 last season.

2. **Terry McLaurin, WAS:** With a final tally of 79 receptions on 132 targets, Terry McLaurin accrued over 1,000 receiving yards in 2023. He found the end zone 4 times, finishing the season with 163.7 fantasy points in half-PPR scoring, which placed him 32nd overall among wide receivers and 41st in points per game (9.6). McLaurin's utilization in the offensive scheme was reflected in his air yards metrics - he held the 23rd spot in air yards share with 35%, emphasizing his role as a deep threat in the Washington pass-happy offense. His total air yards exceeded 1500, ranking him 13th league-wide, a testament to the Commanders' trust in him to stretch the field. While his touchdowns could see an uptick with better quarterback play or offensive scheme changes, his steady reception and yardage totals make him a reliable WR2/3 at worst in 2024. With the No. 2 overall selection Jayden Daniels taking over at QB in Washington (a great deep ball thrower) we could finally see McLaurin break out of the fantasy WR2 quagmire. And he likely won't cost the price of a WR2 in your fantasy football drafts.

3. **Tee Higgins, CIN:** Tee Higgins recorded 42 receptions from 76 targets, covering 656 yards with a notable average of 15.6 yards per reception despite an injury-plagued season. Demonstrating his big-play ability, Higgins had 14 receptions of 20+ yards to go along with a team-high 37% air yards share (17th) on just an 18% target share. He scored 5 touchdowns. Playing in 12 games, Higgins accumulated 116.6 fantasy points, averaging 9.7 points per game (WR40). But he missed games throughout the season and failed to finish as a fantasy WR2 for the first time in the last three seasons. His up-and-down play resulted in a 50% bust rate compared to his 18% bust rate in 2022. Ergo, 2023 stands out as a complete outlier for the 25-year-old WR, who will likely play his last season for the Bengals after being franchise-tagged. The command of air yards shows that Higgins is still a dominant downfield receiver, as are the 4 games where he scored 20-plus fantasy points. Buy the injury discount for a player looking to hit the open market in 2025.

4. **Diontae Johnson, CAR:** Diontae Johnson displayed consistent productivity in 2023, leading the Steelers with a 26% target share, averaging 9.2 fantasy points per game before Week 7. Upon returning from injury Weeks 7-13 (before the Steelers made the switch to Mason Rudolph as QB1), Johnson maintained his effectiveness, securing a 23% target share and scoring 5 touchdowns, averaging 9.7 points per game (36th). Despite changes in quarterback play and his own injuries in Pittsburgh, Johnson remained productive, finishing with 127.2 fantasy points for the season. Now, with the Carolina Panthers, he's poised for a significant target share in an offense that supported Adam Thielen to a WR25 finish, making Johnson a fantasy WR3 with upside, especially if Bryce Young progresses in 2024. The Buccaneers offense – under current Panther head coach Dave Canales – finished second in the NFL last season in WR target share (68%).

5. **Hollywood Brown, KC:** The newest Chiefs WR had a year to forget in 2023. He struggled with bad Arizona Cardinals quarterback play before Kyler Murray returned to the starting lineup as the WR21 overall and as the WR34 in points per game (10.2). But after Murray returned, Hollywood Brown still didn't produce. 5.8 points per game in three full healthy games before ultimately missing the remainder of the season due to injuries. Overall, Brown hauled in 51 receptions on 101 targets, accumulating 574 yards. He scored 109.2 points over the season, averaging 7.8 points per game (53rd) in 13 games played. The lack of production was shocking, considering Brown posted nearly 1,200 air yards, a 25% target share, 85% snap share and 39% air yards share with the 16th-highest weighted opportunity rating. But the future is now, and Hollywood has landed in Kansas City. It's hard to argue against him in the best possible landing spot to resurrect his career with Patrick Mahomes in an offense that needs more playmakers. He can use his speed to stretch the field and be a threat to get the ball, unlike Marquez Valdes-Scantling. But if he hits, it's likely as a fantasy WR2 with his production coming in the early portion of the year, given the potential suspension for Rashee Rice. Brown's season-long upside is somewhat nerfed after the team drafted Xavier Worthy in the first round. While Worthy gets up to "speed" (pun intended), Brown could take advantage. Week 1 is a revenge game for Brown as the Chiefs host the Ravens.

6. **DeAndre Hopkins, TEN:** DeAndre Hopkins showcased his elite receiving skills with 75 catches on 137 targets (28% target share), amassing 1,057 receiving yards in 2023. He proved to be a deep threat with a long reception of 61 yards and 27 catches of 20+ yards. 1,934 total air yards (42%) - the most of any WR during the regular season. Over 17 games, Hopkins scored a total of 186.1 fantasy points, averaging 10.9 points per game (29th), marking him as a dependable WR2 in fantasy lineups. WR22 overall. Specifically, with Will Levis under center, Hopkins posted a 27% target share, 46% air yards share and 13.4 fantasy points per game (WR13). And that came with a sub-50% catch rate. But with Calvin Ridley added to the fold as legitimate target competition, Hopkins' fantasy value takes a hit. He is a bet on cheap volume, but the efficiency may leave a lot to be desired if Levis doesn't progress in his second season. Likely a much better option in PPR formats, where he can tally up receptions in an offense that should be much more pass-happy in the post-Derrick Henry era. Anticipating a friendlier QB system behind an improved offensive line, that much quicker throws will dramatically boost Levis's completion rate in 2024.

7. **Courtland Sutton, DEN:** It's hard to be bullish on Courtland Sutton given his projected outlook with rookie QB Bo Nix, who the Broncos selected in the first round of the 2024 NFL Draft. What we do know is Sutton likely won't benefit from the same TD production for 2 years in a row. 36% of his fantasy points came from TDs – the highest among any top-36 finisher. This past season made amends for 2022 when he couldn't find the end zone. But now that things have leveled out, with a 2-TD season followed by 10 scores in 2023 (14th in red-zone targets), we should project him in the 4-6 TD range for 2024. And that's going to make things tougher on him, because aside from TDs, Sutton's usage wasn't as great as the WR35 overall. In fact, it looks pretty similar to Jerry Jeudy, aside from the TD production (10 vs 2). Both guys had 1,000-plus air yards (36% vs 37%), around 90 targets (21% vs 20%), 750-plus receiving yards, and just under 60 receptions. At least with Jeudy traded to the Browns, that should cement Sutton's floor as the team's projected No. 1 WR, regardless of the QB play. Sutton finished last season as a WR3 in 80% of his games – 7th best among WRs. Sutton has a 23% target share without Jeudy the last 3 seasons. He will compete with second-year WR Marvin Mims and rookie fourth-rounder Troy Franklin, as his main competition for targets. Unless he gets dealt in a trade.

Rookies to Know

1. **Marvin Harrison Jr., ARI:** Marvin Harrison Jr.'s tenure at Ohio State was marked by rapid development, transitioning from a reserved role as a true freshman to a dominant force by his sophomore year. Although given the talent he was competing with for targets as a freshman in 2021 at Ohio State - Chris Olave, Garrett Wilson, Jaxon Smith-Njigba - it's no wonder Harrison couldn't crack the starting lineup. But the 19-year-old finally drew his first start in the Rose Bowl, going nuclear to the tune of 6 catches for 71 yards and 3 TDs. Harrison's junior year further solidified his status as a premier talent, earning him a Heisman Trophy finalist nod-a rare feat for a wide receiver. He concluded the season with 67 receptions for 1,211 yards and 14 TDs. That awarded him not only a 44% dominator rating (second-best mark in the class) but the 2023 Fred Biletnikoff Award bestowed to the best WR in college football. With him entrenched officially as the Arizona Cardinals WR1, he offers a super-high floor with targets and Kyler Murray as his quarterback.

2. **Malik Nabers, NYG:** Malik Nabers, a junior wide receiver from LSU, made significant waves in the college football scene with his impressive 3-year career. Standing at 6 feet and weighing 200 pounds, Nabers led all college wide receivers during the regular season with 86 receptions for 1,546 yards and 14 touchdowns (34% dominator rating). Over his collegiate career, he accumulated 186 receptions for 2,983 yards and 21 touchdowns, showcasing his consistent development and explosive playmaking ability. His 28% career college dominator rating ranks 3rd among all WRs in the 2024 draft class. But what's more impressive is Nabers' age-adjusted production. Broke out at 18 years old in 2021 as a freshman. A great sign of things to come for him with the New York Giants. Nabers can step in from Day 1 as the No. 1 WR in the offense. His explosive skill set as a YAC monster should make drafters less concerned about the potential shoddy QB play from Daniel Jones and/or Drew Lock.

3. **Xavier Worthy, KC:** Xavier Worthy from the University of Texas quickly made a name for himself with his standout speed by breaking the 40-yard dash record at the 2024 NFL Scouting Combine. At 6 feet 1 inch and 172 pounds, Worthy distinguished himself early as a Longhorn, notching 62 receptions for 981 yards and 12 touchdowns in his freshman year. He capped off his college career with over 1,000 yards and 5 touchdowns in his junior year, securing a 30% career dominator rating—the second highest in his class—to go along with an elite breakout age at just 18 years old. His abilities have drawn comparisons to DeSean Jackson, both from Chiefs Head Coach Andy Reid and NFL draft analyst Thor Nystrom, underscoring his potential impact with his new quarterback, Patrick Mahomes. Set to join the Chiefs after being selected in Round 1 of the NFL Draft, Worthy is expected to compete for a significant role, particularly with the possibility of an expanded opportunity if teammate Rashee Rice faces a lengthy early-season suspension.

4. **Ladd McConkey, LAC:** Ladd McConkey isn't without some concerns in his college profile, given his late breakout age at 21 years old. But it was in this third season as a redshirt sophomore (2022) when he totaled 762 receiving yards and seven scores en route to a 20% dominator rating. And be aware that he's been competing with arguably the best college football tight end of all-time in Brock Bowers for targets since he's been at Georgia. And in 2022, Adonai Mitchell (2024 second-round pick) was also a Bulldog but was firmly behind McConkey on the depth chart. In the two games that McConkey played in 2023 without Bowers healthy, he posted his two highest yardage outputs during his final season. The 6-foot 185-pound WR missed games in his final year at Georgia with injuries, which hurt his final counting stats. But he was still uber-efficient, finishing 8th in the nation in yards per route run (3.26). Even so, McConkey's game is characterized by his quickness, route polish, and speed rather than physical dominance. His agility in creating separation and his nuanced route-running skills allow him to find space in tight coverage. He will likely be more underrated than most other WRs based on his final-year stats and injuries. He ran a sub 4.40 40-yard dash at the combine and owned collegiate success at a top program like Georgia. McConkey has the tools to transition effectively to the professional level. The L.A. Chargers traded up with the Patriots to select McConkey. The Chargers depth chart is weak, so we could easily lead them in targets.

5. **Rome Odunze, CHI:** Washington's Rome Odunze's four-year career with the Huskies has been marked by consistent improvement, with his junior year in 2022 marking his status as one of college football's best WRs. 75 catches for 1,145 yards, averaging 15.3 yards per reception, with 7 TDs. The 2023 season saw further improvement, with the 6-foot-3 and 215-pound WR amassing 81 catches for 1,428 yards and 13 TDs, leading to a spot on the AP first team among other awards en route to a career-high 33% dominator rating. And that was accomplished with him battling through a reported broken rib and punctured lung in late September. Overall, he finished with the 4th-highest dominator rating in the 2024 WR class at 26%. Odunze also broke out at the early age of 19 years old, during his sophomore campaign. He was drafted by the Bears 9th overall pairing him to fellow rookie QB Caleb Williams. Odunze will open the season as the Bears WR3 behind veterans Keenan Allen/D.J. Moore, but he could carve out a larger role as the season progresses.

6. **Brian Thomas Jr., JAC:** Brian Thomas Jr. burst onto the scene in his junior year at LSU, demonstrating impressive growth with a 33% dominator rating at 21 years old, leading the FBS with 17 touchdowns, and accumulating 1,177 yards over 68 receptions, at an average of a whopping 17.3 yards per catch. At 6'4" and 209 pounds with a 4.33-second 40-yard dash, he fits the prototype of a boundary X-receiver. Despite not being the primary focus in LSU's offense, Thomas still managed the 6th-highest college dominator rating in his draft class at 24%, often competing for targets with fellow standout and future top-10 pick Malik Nabers. Drafted by the Jaguars in the first round of the 2024 NFL Draft, Thomas is positioned to inherit a significant volume of targets left by Calvin Ridley and Zay Jones, potentially nearing or surpassing 100 targets. If the former LSU WR can absorb the role vacated by Ridley - nearly 1,800 air yards, 22.5% target share, 36% air yards share, NFL leader in end zone targets, WR10 in expected fantasy points per game - Thomas will be one of the best rookies WR targets in fantasy football. However, this might be accompanied by a lack of consistency - given that Thomas doesn't project to be a target alpha in an offense with so many playmakers. There's high-end splash week potential with Thomas in Jacksonville.

7. **Keon Coleman, BUF:** At 6'3" and 213 pounds, Keon Coleman's physicality is undeniable, making him a prototypical outside X-receiver. His junior year performance in his first year at Florida State was noteworthy, with 50 receptions, 658 receiving yards, and 11 touchdowns. 31% dominator rating. But he broke out officially in his sophomore season the year prior at Michigan State, with 58 catches, 798 yards, and seven touchdowns over 12 games. Coleman hung a 29% dominator rating at just 19 years old. And he did this while competing for targets with an older future NFL star in the making, Packers WR Jayden Reed. Coleman had more catches, targets, yards and TDs than the future second-round pick, despite being three years YOUNGER than Reed. Coleman would go on to be the first WR selected in the 2nd round of the 2024 NFL Draft by the Buffalo Bills. Coleman joins a team with a strong quarterback and a depth chart he is well-positioned to climb, suggesting a promising start to his NFL career. The one concern is that Coleman might struggle against press on the outside with the team opting to not deploy him as a big slot (at least early on).

8. **Xavier Legette, CAR:** Xavier Legette, the impactful wide receiver from South Carolina, emerged as a notable talent in college football with his commendable performances, particularly highlighted in his SUPER senior year. Standing at 6'1" and weighing 221 lbs, Legette's physical stature is complemented by his athletic prowess, offering the ideal blend of size and speed required for an outside receiver, making him a formidable presence on the field. One of Legette's most notable qualities is his strong hands - he doesn't use his body to catch the ball - and ability to secure catches in traffic, showcasing his reliability as a target. He broke out in his final and fifth year with the Gamecocks, hanging a 35% dominator rating. He posted 1,255 yards and seven touchdowns on 71 receptions. Entering the league at 23 years old as a one-year wonder raises red flags about Legette's appeal at the next level. The size-speed specimen is enticing, but the lack of consistent production cannot be overlooked. Easy comps for someone with this size and speed are receivers like DK Metcalf, who can often be more situationally dependent as a more "raw" prospect with traits that cannot be taught. Legette's combination of size, catching ability, and consistent playmaking make him an intriguing prospect. He will likely be extremely landing spot-dependent as an obvious boom-or-bust WR. Legette was drafted in the 1st round by the Carolina Panthers, who traded

into Round 1 to select him. Expect new HC Dave Canales to take advantage of Legette's game that is tied to designed plays and yards after the catch.

9. **Ricky Pearsall, SF:** Ricky Pearsall broke out at Arizona State in his third season with a 28% dominator rating in 2021, tallying 580 yards and 4 TDs. Future No. 2 overall pick, Jayden Daniels, was his starting QB after a 2020 season that was limited to four games due to the pandemic. After transferring to the SEC, the 6-foot-1 and 189-pound WR continued to succeed over the next two years at Florida, with dominator ratings of 25% from 2022-2023, finishing with 963 receiving yards and 4 TDs in his final season as a Gator. In 2022, he was Anthony Richardson's No. 1 WR and out-produced future NFL draft pick, Justin Shorter. He averaged nearly 20 yards per catch as the team's slot WR. Still, he's an older prospect, considering he will be 24 years old this season. The other concern is how he can separate himself from his future NFL teammates when it comes to his target competition. His target share over expectation (0.9%) ranked 36th in the class. Even so, he turned heads at the NFL Scouting Combine with strong metrics across the board. 4.41 40-yard dash, 42" vertical jump, 129" broad jump, 4.05 20-yard shuttle (89th percentile) and 6.64 3-cone drill (93rd percentile). Pearsall's experience as a fifth-year senior, round 1 draft capital and refined game makes him a high-floor player who can produce from the get-go, but he may not have any more ceiling to unlock unless he lands with a truly elite NFL passer. So even though Slick Rick hit the jackpot on Night 1 of the NFL Draft with first-round draft capital in the 49ers offense that schemes WRs in the best way and takes advantage of their strengths... I am somewhat skeptical of how high Pearsall's ceiling is. Especially if Deebo Samuel/ Brandon Aiyuk remain on the roster throughout the 2024 season. Pearsall needs this depth chart to open up to produce in Year 1.

10. **Jermaine Burton, CIN:** Jermaine Burton took forever to "break out" until his senior year at 22 years old with a 30% dominator rating as a member of the Crimson Tide. He transferred from the University of Georgia over his first two seasons to Alabama for his final two collegiate seasons. Although he did post a very serviceable 19% dominator rating his first year at Bama (essentially a breakout), with 677 yards and 7 TDs. Burton also produced decently during his time in Georgia despite facing a myriad of tough competition. 16% dominator rating in 2020 as a true freshman (19 years old) while competing for targets with future NFL pro George Pickens. During his second season as a Bulldog, Burton was second on the team in receiving yards behind only Brock Bowers - despite competing for targets with the aforementioned tight end, Ladd McConkey and Adonai Mitchell (more NFL talent). He was also used exclusively downfield during his final year, with a 20.2 aDOT (3rd-highest in the FBS) in 2023. And zero drops. Burton also led all WRs in the 2024 class and finished 12th overall in yards per route run. Burton possesses an explosive skill set with 4.45 wheels and jumps in the 82nd percentile-plus. He's a big play waiting to happen, but likely won't command a hyper-intense target share at the next level. He has only two games on his college resume with double-digit targets. Burton also has some off-field issue concerns that could have impacted his draft capital in the real-life NFL. But the Bengals still felt confident enough to draft him in Round 3, which bodes well for his NFL future. Because the writing is on the wall that Tee Higgins is not in the Bengals' long-term plans. Whether Higgins gets moved this year or next offseason, Burton's stock will be on a steady rise from here on out, assuming his off-field issues don't get in his way.

11. **Javon Baker, NE:** Javon Baker couldn't sniff the field at Alabama (he wanted the ball), so he transferred to UCF during the last two seasons of his college tenure. He enjoyed two strong seasons with the Knights, posting dominator ratings of 23% and 31%. The 6-foot-1 and 202-pound WR was a big-play savant, owning the second-highest yards per reception (21.9) nationally in 2023. He ended the season 5th in yards per route run among the 2024 WR draft class (3.21). Stylistically, Baker has shades of DeVonta Smith from a route-running and body control perspective. Makes sense, given Baker learned under Smith during his Crimson Tide days. But Baker has more size and YAC to his game. He was drafted by the Patriots in Rd 4, but could make some noise on a relatively weak depth chart. Even though the Patriots drafted Washington's Ja'Lynn Polk two rounds ahead of Baker, he offers a much higher ceiling as a potential alpha. Baker finished fourth in targets and third in receptions of 20-plus air yards in 2023. The only other WRs in the class to do so? The consensus top-four (Harrison Jr., Odunze, Thomas Jr. and Malik Nabers).

12. **Troy Franklin, DEN:** By his junior season in 2023, Troy Franklin had established himself as a premier college football receiver, amassing nearly 1,400 yards and 14 touchdowns, demonstrating not just his ability to find the end zone but also his ceiling with a final season dominator rating of 29% - 17th-highest mark in the 2024 class. Franklin's strengths lie in his speed, with a rumored 40-yard dash time of 4.35 seconds, making him a formidable deep threat with 14 catches of 20-plus air yards and the third-highest yards per route run (3.32) in the 2024 draft class. Despite concerns about his slender frame, his selection by the Broncos in Round 4, facilitated by Sean Payton's history of trading up for receivers, positions him for significant playing time. Reuniting with former college quarterback Bo Nix enhances Franklin's potential impact in Denver's offense, potentially overshadowing fellow receiver Marvin Mims. With Payton eyeing Franklin for a key role and his established chemistry with Nix, he could quickly establish himself as an asset for the Broncos. Franklin's fall from a fringe 1st-round pick to Day 3 isn't ideal, but in another year where WR wasn't as deep he likely would have gone earlier. Other teams were scared off due to his poor combine showing and slight frame. And more importantly, he lands on a relatively weak WR depth chart where his 4th-round pedigree won't hinder his playing time. Payton envisions Franklin in the "Z" role, which was occupied by Jerry Jeudy last season. And if you are Nix, seems likely you'll prefer your old college teammate you've built chemistry with the past several years than a second-year WR that struggled to earn playing time/targets as a rookie.

13. **Adonai Mitchell, IND:** As a Longhorn, Adonai "AD" Mitchell posted a breakout season en route to a 32 percent dominator rating with 11 TD scores on 55 receptions. Standing at 6'2" with a 205-pound frame, Mitchell offers an ideal build for an outside receiver. Mitchell mirrors a lighter Michael Pittman Jr. based on his film. At the NFL Combine, he had a big day: 4.34-second 40-yard dash (94th percentile), 1.52-second 10-yard split (76th percentile), 39.5" vertical jump (89th percentile), 136" broad jump (98th percentile). His closest comparable per mockdraftable.com is D.J. Chark Jr. After being drafted by the Colts in the 2nd round, Mitchell projects to take on Alec Pierce's role in the Shane Steichen offense. Pierce ranked 17th in route participation last season (84%) and second in total snaps per game (64, 95%). As an explosive vertical threat, Mitchell's game could translate well to second-year QB Anthony Richardson's big arm. But in an offense heralded by a mobile quarterback, Mitchell is facing an uphill battle for total targets. Pittman Jr is the target alpha. And last year's second-round pick, Josh Downs, projects for No. 2 in the target pecking order. Mitchell screams like the 3rd-target at best, with his opportunities mostly coming in the form of downfield and high-value pass attempts. It's great in best ball for splash weeks. But relying on Mitchell to bring in any consistency is a fool's errand.

14. **Roman Wilson, PIT:** At 5'10" and 185 pounds, Roman Wilson combines athletic prowess with technical skill to make an impact on the field. He truly saved his best for last in Michigan's run for the national championship. His standout senior year saw him amassing 48 receptions for 789 yards and 12 touchdowns, resulting in a 37% dominator rating in 2023. It was the 6th-highest single-season dominator rating in the class. The obvious concerns are his late breakout age at 22 years old and the fact that he could only muster one legitimate year of production. Even so, he was turning heads at the most recent Senior Bowl, and his stock has continued to rise after running a sub-4.40 yard-dash at the 2024 NFL Scouting Combine. He's drawn comparisons to Tyler Lockett from the Senior Bowl's own Jim Nagy. No doubt that's related to his deep prowess, given that 53% of his routes were downfield per Sports Info Solutions. But given that the Steelers project to be extremely run-heavy after the hiring of OC Arthur Smith - in addition to the draft selections of OL Zach Frazier and OL Troy Fautanu - I'm finding it hard to be excited about Wilson (a real-life NFL 3rd-round draft pick) for fantasy purposes. Fading a Steelers mid-round WR selection is always a risky proposition, but I'm not finding many ways where not drafting Wilson buries me in 2024.

15. **Ja'Lynn Polk, NE:** Ja'Lynn Polk, the talented No. 2 wide receiver from Washington, made a notable mark in college football with his performances, particularly shining in his junior year. With a height of 6'1" and weighing in at 203 lbs, Polk has the ideal build for a versatile receiver capable of playing both on the outside and in the slot. In his time at Washington, Polk demonstrated significant growth, culminating in a senior year after suffering an injury as a sophomore. He recorded impressive stats with 69 receptions for 1,159 yards and nine touchdowns, boasting a massive 16.8 yards per catch. He also started the 2023 season on absolute fire, scoring eight TDs in the first 10 weeks of the season alongside a teammate and future top-10 draft pick, WR Rome Odunze. Reminds me of Mohamed Sanu and Tyler Boyd. Other NFL Draft evaluators have compared Polk to Joshua Palmer. Selected in the second round of the 2024 NFL Draft by the Patriots, he is poised to become a dependable part of their passing game.

16. **Jalen McMillan, TB:** Jalen McMillan broke out in his second season at Washington at 20 years old. He compiled a 19% dominator rating which set the stage for what was coming for him in 2022 when he had his best college season with 1,098 receiving yards and 9 TDs. Good for a 25% dominator rating despite competing for targets with future NFL WRs Rome Odunze and Ja'Lynn Polk. He led the Huskies in targets and catches in 2022 despite playing with future 1st and 2nd round picks. Alas, he could not sustain that success into this past season as the No. 3 option in Washington's pass attack given his injury and lack of usage downfield (9.6 average depth of target) in a vertical passing attack. It won't get easier to command targets in Tampa Bay. But the fact that McMillan showed he's capable of rising to the occasion of elite target competition bodes well for him in the long-term or should injury strike Mike Evans/Chris Godwin. The former Huskie is a strong route runner with an early breakout age. He has played over 89% of the snaps from the slot over the last two seasons. Odds are that one of McMillan or Polk will perform WELL above expectation at the next level, given how they likely hurt each other's statistics the past two seasons with Washington's spread offense. McMillan was drafted by the Buccaneers in the 3rd-round of this year's draft. McMillan can step in as the WR3 as soon as this season, and WR2 is within his reach come 2025 should the team move on from Godwin in the final year of his contract.

17. **Luke McCaffrey, WAS:** Christian McCaffrey's brother was the final pick in Round 3 by the Washington Commanders. They needed a slot WR, and the younger Luke McCaffrey can fill that void in Kliff Kingsbury's offense. McCaffrey has not been playing WR for very long but possesses elite athletic bloodlines that have helped him make the switch. Usually, it's not wise to chase the draft capital of WRs that go well ahead of mock draft consensus, but McCaffrey's late Round 3/Day 2 draft capital should put fantasy managers on notice. In his final season at Rice, he commanded a 30% target share (5th in the class) and ranked 9th in total unique routes run. Given the uncertainty on the depth chart among pass-catchers behind Terry McLaurin in the nation's capital, don't sleep on McCaffrey.

18. **Malik Washington, MIA:** Malik Washington, standing at 5-foot-8 and weighing 191 pounds, made a significant impact in his final college season at Virginia, after transferring from Northwestern. He achieved an impressive 47% dominator rating, led the 2024 draft class with a 38% target share, and accumulated nearly 1,400 receiving yards and 9 touchdowns, earning him the second-highest PFF grade of 92.4 among WRs. His 2023 season was one of the best in the class. Washington's exceptional performance continued into the NFL Combine, where he led his class with a 42.5-inch vertical jump (98th percentile), showcasing his remarkable athleticism despite his shorter stature. Drafted by the Dolphins in the sixth round, his skills as a YAC (yards after catch) specialist make him a promising addition to an offense that already features dynamic playmakers like Tyreek Hill and Jaylen Waddle. Coach Mike McDaniel's enthusiasm for Washington (he was bugging his general manager to draft him several rounds earlier) suggests he could significantly exceed expectations, benefiting from both opportunity and a quarterback capable of enhancing his fantasy production. Odell Beckham Jr.'s presence shouldn't stop Washington if he's truly a viable piece on offense.

Matchup Plays

1. **Jameson Williams, DET:** Jameson Williams has had a tumultuous two years in the NFL. His rookie year was lost because of a torn ACL, and the 2023 season started out slow because of a suspension. When he's been on the field, he's teased big-play upside with a lot of inconsistencies and injuries. Entering Year 3, the former first-rounder will likely be viewed as a logical breakout candidate. After all, the WR2 job should be all his with Josh Reynolds signing with the Denver Broncos. But Williams is hardly without his warts with just a 10% target share earned, 15% target rate per route run, and 6.4 points per game scored in 2023 (WR66 same as Reynolds). Williams might be overrated heading into 2024 because of his draft capital from two years ago. And everything he showed in his second season suggests he still has a long way to go, especially as the "at best" third or fourth receiving option on the Lions. At this year's NFL Scouting Combine, Lions HC Dan Campbell praised Williams's growth in 2023 but claimed he's going to "push" for a full-time starting job. It's Year 3, and we don't even have a full role locked in for Williams? Good grief.

2. **Jahan Dotson, WAS:** Curtis Samuel signed with the Bills in free agency. This is important because it suggests that we could have hope for Jahan Dotson in Year 3. Dotson broke out as a rookie but was an utter bust in 2023. And he ran all the routes you could possibly ask for in the Commanders' pass-happy offense. Garrett Wilson and teammate Terry McLaurin were the only guys who ran more routes than Dotson did in 2023. He was brutally inefficient - as was the entire Washington passing game that was more volume over efficiency - finishing bottom-10 in yards per route run. But Samuel missed or played very little in 3 games in 2023 - Weeks 8,9, and 11. These were by FAR Dotson's best games. 15.2 points per game with a TD scored in all 3 contests. Dotson was narrowly out-targeted by McLaurin as the No. 2 WR. Both McLaurin and Dotson need a C.J. Stroud-level impact from No.2 overall pick, Jayden Daniels, for them to take any leap for fantasy football. Be mindful that Dotson saw more red-zone targets than McLaurin in 2023.

3. **Curtis Samuel, BUF:** Curtis Samuel finished the 2023 season as the WR44 overall, averaging 7.9 fantasy points per game as the WR52 in points per game (7.9) in his final season with the Washington Commanders. Par for the course when it comes to Samuel, who always seems to string together consecutive weeks of production before seeing his numbers drop off because of injury. His receiving numbers were nearly identical to his 2020 campaign, albeit he was more efficient as Washington's primary slot WR. Unfortunately, he was barely used as a rusher with only 7 carries compared to 38 in 2022. Entering his age 28 season, Samuel has never finished higher than WR25 at any point during his career, regulating him to WR4 fantasy status, barring extreme circumstances. He will have his fair share of productive weeks, but nothing to move the needle as a fantasy game-changer. However, it needs to be noted his best season came in 2020 with the Carolina Panthers under Joe Brady, his new OC in Buffalo. In Samuel's last year with Brady in Carolina, he played 72% of his snaps from the slot. Attached to Josh Allen in a full-time role, Samuel has nice sleeper appeal in the Bills offense, especially with Stefon Diggs and Gabe Davis gone from the offense.

4. **Jakobi Meyers, LV:** Jakobi Meyers' underrated talent was on full display all season in 2023, as the first-year Raider scored 8 receiving TDs (10 total) on a 21% target share and 15 red-zone targets (23rd). After failing comically to find the end zone as a member of the Patriots for most of his tenure spent in New England, Meyers couldn't stop scoring in 2023. This will likely regress next season as he scored four more TDs over expectation. Meyers accumulated 183.1 fantasy points over the season, resulting in an average of 11.4 points per game, ranking him 25th among wide receivers in points per game. Meyers was also the WR25 with Aidan O'Connell from Weeks 9-18, averaging 10.4 fantasy points per game (33rd). There are question marks about how effective Meyers will be in 2024 with Gardner Minshew added at quarterback, and first-round tight end Brock Bowers drafted as another dynamic pass-catcher. Although the target competition won't likely be enough to remove Meyers from the fantasy WR3 conversation, given his three straight finishes as a top-30 fantasy WR. The Raiders WR was also a top-36 WR in expected points per game in 2023. His ceiling may not be as high as it was last year, but it comes with strong value based on his low projected draft position.

5. **Mike Williams, NYJ:** Mike Williams' signing with the Jets on a one-year, $15 million deal provides a temporary solution at the wide receiver position, albeit with some concerns given his age and recent injury history. Despite his Week 3 ACL tear, Williams had been productive prior to the injury, ranking as WR15 overall and WR17 in points per game. His addition gives the Jets a veteran presence and much-needed/immediate depth behind Garrett Wilson. But let's not get carried away with his individual accolades in last year's small sample size. It's the same story every year with Big Mike. WR20 in points per game in 2022 but missed four games. At this point, it seems Williams will never fully put together a truly epic WR1 season that he has teased every year since 2018. He's effective enough when healthy to post massive weeks that we know will not endure the length of the season. Translation? You draft Williams with the sole purpose of selling high. Because with Aaron Rodgers as his QB, Williams is slated to have his fair share of TD-boosted fantasy spike weeks.

6. **Joshua Palmer, LAC:** It's difficult not to view Josh Palmer as a legitimate winner this offseason after the Chargers moved on from both Mike Williams and Keenan Allen. Palmer stepped up big time in the Chargers anemic offense last season when Williams and Allen missed time. In Week 18, he commanded 10 targets despite running on a 58% snap share. During the season, he posted an 18% target share and averaged 1.89 yards per route run. In games played without Williams fully healthy, Palmer averaged 10.6 points per game. During the final three games of the year with neither top WR nor Justin Herbert available, Palmer hit a 20% target share and 23% target rate per route run averaging 11.5 points per game (WR25). The Chargers drafted Ladd McConkey at the top of the 2nd round, so don't go crazy with Palmer. But note that he is still a solid in-house option on the roster that has built-in chemistry with Herbert. Hardly the case with Quentin Johnston after his abysmal rookie season. Also, it should be recognized that McConkey was never the marquee bill of health during his college tenure. Should the rookie miss time Palmer would reap the rewards.

7. **Josh Downs, IND:** Josh Downs made a notable impact in his rookie season with 68 receptions from 98 targets (17% target share), totaling 771 yards, averaging 11.3 yards per reception. Note that he was very unlucky when it came to scoring, with just two TDs. Only Falcons WR Drake London had more receiving yards and fewer than 3 TDs than Downs did in 2023. As a result, over 17 games, he amassed 123.1 fantasy points, averaging 7.2 points per game (WR46). But it should be made known that Downs' production fell off after he suffered a knee injury that lingered throughout the season. Weeks 1-8, Downs led the Colts in yards per route run (2.0), averaging 9.9 points per game with a 19% target share. He is sure to be overlooked after the Colts drafted another WR in Round 2 with Texas WR Adonai Mitchell.

8. **Jerry Jeudy, CLE:** Jerry Jeudy showcased his route running finesse and quickness, turning his 54 receptions on 87 targets into 758 receiving yards, averaging 14 yards per catch in 2023. However, finding the end zone was less frequent for Jeudy, with only 2 touchdowns to his name. He was completely outshined by teammate Courtland Sutton in this capacity. Over the season, Jeudy accumulated 114.8 fantasy points, coming out to an average of 7.2 points per game to a WR50 overall finish. Both Sutton and Jeudy had 1,000-plus air yards (36% vs 37%), around 90 targets (21% vs 20%), 750-plus receiving yards, and just under 60 receptions. Hard to see Jeudy breaking even the fantasy WR3 mold in his first season with the Cleveland Browns unless we get elite QB play from Deshaun Watson, in addition to the newcomer playing/earning a full-time role. Based on the contract Jeudy signed - 3 years and $52.5 million – it's his job to lose as the WR2 versus Elijah Moore, who will be entering the last year of his rookie contract.

9. **Rashid Shaheed, NO:** Rashid Shaheed demonstrated his big-play ability during his 2nd season, accumulating over 1,000 air yards on just 75 targets, showcasing his knack for explosive receptions. Despite a modest 14% target share, Shaheed ranked 14th with 31 catches of 20-plus yards, highlighting his propensity for game-changing plays. With 132.6 fantasy points scored, he averaged 8.3 points per game, securing the 49th spot among wide receivers in points per game. Over the last 19 games he has played alongside Chris Olave, Shaheed has averaged 53.5 receiving yards per game compared to Olave's 66.3. Shaheed also had more top-12 finishes (3) than Olave (2) in 2023.

10. **Khalil Shakir, BUF:** Khalil Shakir tied a bow on his second season on an extremely high note. He showed up big in the absence of the now-departed Gabe Davis, catching 16 of 17 targets for 180 yards and 2 TDs over the last three games of the season. Shakir finished the season with the NFL's highest catch rate (88%) and passer rating generated (141.5). Super-efficient. He also led the Bills in receiving EPA, and ranked 16th overall in that category among all NFL receivers. He has "earned" a bigger role in the offense in 2024, but he will still have to compete for targets with second-round rookie, Keon Coleman and veteran newcomers such as Curtis Samuel, Mack Hollins and Marquez Valdes-Scantling. Given that Shakir is best deployed from the slot, he might need a Samuel injury to unlock his full potential in 2024.

11. **Romeo Doubs, GB:** Romeo Doubs followed up on a decent rookie campaign with an improved second season. He was a consistent presence in the Packers' passing game, recording 69 receptions on 105 targets for 908 yards. Doubs found the end zone 9 times, proving to be a valuable red zone target. Over 19 games, he averaged 9.4 points per game (WR47), making him a solid WR4 in fantasy leagues. He benefitted greatly from TDs and injuries to other primary Packers pass-catchers. Worth noting that he also failed to take full advantage of the vast opportunity in the offense, scoring fewer than his expected output (11.1 per game). This creates some concerns about his 2024 potential given his production could tail off if players like Christian Watson are healthy in Green Bay's offense.

12. **Dontayvion Wicks, GB:** While Christian Watson missed time, 2023 5th-round rookie Dontayvion Wicks stepped up. He caught 39 passes from 58 targets for 581 yards at 14.9 yards per reception during the regular season. He displayed big-play capability with a long catch of 35 yards and 14 receptions over 20 yards. Wicks scored 5 touchdowns (including postseason), and scored 100.3 fantasy points over 15 games, averaging 6.7 points per game. The 6-foot-1 and 206-pound WR averaged nearly 2.0 yards per route run – which ranked 27th among all WRs and 5th among all rookies. It was also nearly identical to Jayden Reed's yards per route run. Given Jordan Love's tendency to spread the "love" between his pass-catchers, Wicks is a super deep sleeper who could emerge as one of the top pass-catchers in this ascending Packers offense.

13. **Darnell Mooney, ATL:** Darnell Mooney is coming off a horrible and injury-plagued 2023 season, but that made him a STEAL as a free agent for the Falcons. Mooney finished the season 10th in yards after the catch per reception (6.0) despite entering the year coming off a late November 2022 broken ankle injury. Mooney shined his brightest from 2021-2022 in the NFL with a 27% target share. He has shown the ability to command targets at a high level. In Atlanta, there is nobody behind Drake London, cementing Mooney as the clear-cut WR2 in a Kirk Cousins-led offense. The targets might be hard to come by on the surface, but a pass-happy offense can potentially feed more than one weapon. One also must consider Atlanta was extremely healthy on offense last year, which tends to regress annually. If someone goes down in this Falcons offense, expect Mooney's fantasy value to launch to the moon.

14. **Brandin Cooks, DAL:** Brandin Cooks ended the season as the WR45 in points per game (9.1) and WR36 overall. After his sluggish start, Cooks was unlocked from Week 6 onward as we saw the Dallas offense start to click. WR22 overall and WR28 in points per game (11.2). But be warned that Cooks is coming off the worst YAC/reception of his career (2.3) and the worst yards per route run of his career (1.19). He will be 31 in September.

15. **Gabe Davis, JAC:** Gabriel Davis did not play in the final two games of the Bills' season. The 2024 free agent signed with the Jaguars this offseason. He finished the season as the WR40 in total points, averaging 8.2 points per game as the WR50. Davis posted 5 games with 20-plus fantasy points in 2023 to go along with 7 TDs and 1,200 air yards (30th), but he also went completely catchless in four of his last 8 games played. Even on a Jacksonville depth chart where he could theoretically improve on his 2023 15% target share (85th) given the departures of Zay Jones and Calvin Ridley, Davis' body of work as a boom-or-bust player will be hard to knock. One could argue that he's also taking a step back with Trevor Lawrence as his new QB. Therefore, his spiked weeks might also not be nearly as big even if he is slightly more consistent on a week-to-week basis (fingers crossed). The latter is also hardly a lock, given the depth the Jaguars have across their several established pass-catchers. They also drafted a better/younger version of Davis in Round 1 of the draft, in the form of LSU's Brian Thomas Jr. Better in best ball? Yup.

16. **Zay Jones, ARI:** Zay Jones had a moderate impact for the Jaguars in 2023 with 34 receptions on 64 targets, gathering just 321 yards at an average of 9.4 yards per reception. He was hurt the entire season with three different injuries, so I'd call his 2023 campaign a wash. Playing in 9 games, he earned 61.1 fantasy points with 2 TDs, averaging 6.8 points per game. WR62 in points per game. I'd look more at his final four games as a better representation of what we can expect from a healthy Jones. Without Kirk, Jones averaged 8 fantasy points per game and 17.3 expected points per game. He saw target totals of 8, 14, 8 and 9. Similar to Calvin Ridley, there was a stark difference between expected and actual production. He was released by the Jaguars after the 2024 NFL Draft but wasn't on the open market for very long, immediately inking with the Arizona Cardinals. Inside the dome with Kyler Murray as his QB, Jones has some spike week appeal given the "highs" he showed during his time spent when healthy in Jacksonville.

17. **Odell Beckham Jr., MIA:** Odell Beckham just turned 31 years old and did not live up to his contract expectations as a Baltimore Raven in 2023. He was the WR63 overall, averaging 6.4 fantasy points per game (WR67). However, he still had his moments averaging 1.8 yards per route run - identical to his averages during his time spent in Cleveland from 2019-2020. He was a top-30 WR in PFF receiving grade with a top-3 ADOT among WRs as a primary deep threat in the Ravens' offense. And once OBJ got his sea legs under him - after Week 8 - he started to show out more. 18th in yards per route run (2.3). He's not completely washed and still can provide some fantasy juice in a favorable offensive environment. He signed a 1-year deal with the Dolphins this offseason and will likely be deployed in the most efficient way possible, giving him some fantasy appeal in specific matchups and/or an injury hits Miami's WR depth chart.

Chapter 7

Tight Ends

Evan Tarracciano

	TE1 PPR		
	Player	RPV	$
1	Travis Kelce	30%	28
2	Sam LaPorta	18%	21
3	Trey McBride	8%	14
4	Kyle Pitts	8%	12
5	Mark Andrews	6%	12
6	Evan Engram	-1%	10
7	George Kittle	-4%	10
8	Dalton Kincaid	-6%	9
9	Brock Bowers	-9%	9
10	David Njoku	-15%	8
11	Cole Kmet	-16%	7
12	Jake Ferguson	-21%	5

	TE2 PPR	
	Player	RPV
13	Dallas Goedert	28%
14	Dalton Schultz	24%
15	Pat Freiermuth	3%
16	Taysom Hill	1%
17	T.J. Hockenson	-1%
18	Tyler Conklin	-4%
19	Hunter Henry	-4%
20	Jonnu Smith	-5%
21	Cade Otton	-5%
22	Isaiah Likely	-5%
23	Luke Musgrave	-14%
24	Darren Waller	-18%

	TE1 STND		
	Player	Proj FPTS	RPV
1	Travis Kelce	180	47%
2	Sam LaPorta	150	22%
3	Mark Andrews	130	6%
4	Trey McBride	130	6%
5	Kyle Pitts	120	-2%
6	George Kittle	115	-6%
7	Evan Engram	115	-6%
8	David Njoku	110	-10%
9	Dalton Kincaid	109	-11%
10	Taysom Hill	107	-13%
11	Cole Kmet	105	-14%
12	Jake Ferguson	100	-18%

	TE2 STND	
	Player	RPV
13	Brock Bowers	43%
14	Dalton Schultz	40%
15	Dallas Goedert	24%
16	Pat Freiermuth	4%
17	T.J. Hockenson	-4%
18	Tyler Conklin	-7%
19	Hunter Henry	-7%
20	Jonnu Smith	-10%
21	Cade Otton	-12%
22	Isaiah Likely	-15%
23	Luke Musgrave	-19%
24	Darren Waller	-38%

Get updated RPV Cheat Sheets 10 & 12 tm leagues for one time $5 cost (free updates) PayPal: FantasyBlackBook@gmail.com or Venmo: @FantasyBlackBook And include your email address

Historically speaking, the tight end position has offered two options for fantasy managers. Select a top-tier player within the elite upper echelon of the first few rounds or punt the position until later in the draft in favor of a committee or streaming approach. Thankfully, that "option A or B" approach is dwindling due to the abundance of mid-tier options that are not entirely dependent upon catching a touchdown each week. A recent youth movement at the quarterback position across the league has made tight ends more relevant, mainly due to their routes being run closer to the line of scrimmage, coupled with the defensive attention that wide receivers draw.

While an elite tier of tight ends still exists, fantasy managers now have the option to select a 'set it and forget it' player later in drafts, avoiding the need to spend precious waiver wire priority adds or FAAB bids to stream the position. Last season, the performance of nine tight ends with more than 70 receptions or 700 receiving yards and six players who finished with more than 200 fantasy points in a PPR format further underscored this trend. But the thrilling part-rookie tight ends are now making a faster impact in fantasy football, thanks to colleges adopting pro-style offenses more frequently. For instance, last season's top scorer was rookie Sam LaPorta from Detroit, who outperformed veterans Evan Engram and Travis Kelce. He became the first rookie to achieve overall TE1 status in 35 years since Keith Jackson in 1988. Another rookie, Dalton Kincaid, was just outside the top-10. The future of your fantasy team could be in the hands of these rookies, sparking hope and excitement for the season ahead.

Similar to the quarterback position, there are various strategies you can adopt when it comes to drafting tight ends. To secure a weekly statistical advantage, you can address the position early in the draft. However, if you prefer a more balanced approach, waiting until the mid-rounds to select the TE5-TE14 is a perfectly viable option. This flexibility in drafting strategies allows you to tailor your team to your needs and preferences.

Elite

1. **Sam LaPorta, DET**: LaPorta shook the long-held stigma that rookie tight ends are irrelevant for fantasy and need an entire redshirt season to acclimate to the league's demands. In 2023, he averaged nearly 53 receiving yards per game and led the position with ten touchdowns. Red zone regression is a distinct possibility, but we anticipate his target volume will remain strong with Jared Goff under center in Detroit. LaPorta's athleticism creates mismatches all over the field, and he is a perfect fit for coordinator Ben Johnson's offense. His ceiling is immense.

2. **Travis Kelce, KC**: The unanimous TE1 overall for the last half-decade, Kelce took a statistical step backward in 2023, failing to eclipse the 1,000-yard receiving mark for the first time since 2015, and his five touchdowns were the lowest total since 2019. Additionally, offseason acquisitions to the Chief's bolstered receiving room in Marquise Brown and Xavier Worthy will erode Kelce's usually overwhelming target share. Kelce's chemistry with quarterback Patrick Mahomes is undeniable, but his time in the sun is fading as he enters the season at 34 years old. He remains a top pick at the position amidst a dynasty in Kansas City.

3. **Trey McBride, ARI**: McBride's minimal usage in the first half of last season did little to suggest that a significant breakout was on the horizon. Ranked as the TE30 after week seven, he went ballistic after veteran Zach Ertz was placed on IR with a quad injury, reminding the nation why he won the prestigious Mackey Award in 2021. Featured as the alpha receiving option for Arizona, McBride finished with a strong 81/825/3 stat line, placing him at TE6 in 2023. Rookie wideout Marvin Harrison Jr. will push McBride into Kyler Murray's second read on most passing situations. Still, he has entrenched himself within the highest tier at the position on an ascending offense.

4. **Mark Andrews, BAL** – Andrews was off to another phenomenal start last year before an ankle injury in Week 11 ended his season prematurely. A top-five talent when healthy, it is the "when healthy" caveat that has plagued Andrews since his breakout 2019 season. He recorded an entire season just once during that span, leaving fantasy managers constantly wondering what could have been. He remains the top red-zone passing threat for Lamar Jackson, thanks to his fantastic hands and large catch radius. If Andrews can finally elude the injury bug for the entirety of 2024, he poses a real threat to finish as the top overall player at the position, even in a run-heavy Baltimore scheme. A repeat of his epic 2021 season (107/1,361/9) is still within reach, but setting proper expectations and reinforcing the position with a high-upside backup would be wise.

Top Targets

1. **Dalton Kincaid, BUF:** Kincaid made headlines as the first tight end selected in the 2023 NFL Draft, and at first glance, his final statistics were solid – 73 receptions on 91 targets for 673 yards and two touchdowns. However, his weekly production was erratic, mainly due to the offensive philosophy shift mid-season with the firing of coordinator Ken Dorsey, coupled with the presence of Dawson Knox. When Knox was sidelined with a wrist injury over a five-game stretch midseason, Kincaid flourished, and his production nearly doubled. Knox's subsequent return relegated Kincaid to streaming status instead. Buffalo's salary cap woes forced the team to let several major contributors go, including both top receivers Stefon Diggs and Gabe Davis. Florida State standout Keon Coleman will soak up some of those targets, but Kincaid should see an overall expanded role resulting from the changes. His elite athletic profile and ability to generate YAC will make him a focal point for Josh Allen in 2024.

2. **George Kittle, SF:** Fantasy managers who draft Kittle live by the old Darkwing Duck motto, "Let's get dangerous." Through no fault of his own, Kittle's weekly point totals are Jekyll and Hyde, mainly due to the plethora of weapons the 49ers have on offense and their tendency to lean on the running game when ahead. Last season, Kittle had ten games with three or fewer receptions, and he scored just three touchdowns after his outburst in Week 5 – difficult totals to swallow for fantasy players involved in close contests. Few players are more explosive when utilized as a focal point in the passing attack. Kittle's 15.7 YPC in 2023 was light years ahead of his TE1 counterparts, mainly due to his violent running style that seeks to run through defenders after contact. San Francisco's embarrassment of riches on offense will result in Kittle having low target volume again, so he must make the most of every pass thrown his way.

3. **Kyle Pitts, ATL:** Could this be the season that Pitts finally breaks out for Atlanta? The tight end "prince that was promised" entered the league in 2021 with great fanfare and appeared to be the next big star, posting a 68-catch, 1,026-yard season. The following two years were marred by a torn MCL, damage to his PCL, and being forced to play under head coach Arthur Smith – the equivalent of latrine duty for playmakers. Thankfully, the Falcons fired Smith in the offseason, and Pitts fully recovered from his knee injury and is now fully healthy. The Falcons brought in Zac Robinson (formerly the passing game coordinator in Los Angeles) as their new offensive coordinator and signed Kirk Cousins to a multi-year contract. The stars have aligned for Pitts to produce at a much higher level, and he should come at a discount in drafts after two disappointing seasons.

4. **Evan Engram, JAC:** After five disappointing seasons in New York, Engram joined the Jaguars in 2022 and has blossomed into a significant part of the team's offense. In each of the past two seasons, he has set new career highs in receptions and receiving yards, developing into a reliable option for Trevor Lawrence. Engram led all tight ends with 114 receptions last year on 143 targets and was primarily used as a chain-moving option and security blanket under duress. Unlike others at the position, Engram has a healthy weekly floor due to his target share, but his fantasy ceiling is capped since he isn't Jacksonville's primary red zone option. The Jaguars' deep receiving core (Christian Kirk, Gabe Davis, and rookie Brian Thomas Jr.) will make it difficult for Engram to surpass his 2023 totals.

5. **David Njoku, CLE:** Njoku finished as the TE5 last year after setting new single-season highs in receptions (81), receiving yards (882), and touchdowns (6). The biggest beneficiary of the midseason switch from Deshaun Watson to Joe Flacco, Njoku quickly became the primary read on many passing plays rather than the third option behind Amari Cooper and Elijah Moore. Fantasy managers now need to asses if Njoku will continue to have an expanded role after showing Cleveland that he is more than capable or if he will return to a supplementary role instead. During the first five games of 2023 with Watson under center, Njoku averaged just four receptions and 35 yards per game – numbers need to improve to justify his ranking within this territory.

Solid Options

1. **Jake Ferguson, DAL:** After Dalton Schultz left the Cowboys in favor of the in-state Houston Texans, Ferguson seamlessly shifted into the void and finished with 71 receptions for 761 yards and five touchdowns. Drafted as a streaming option outside the top 24 tight ends, Ferguson finished as the TE9 and provided fantasy managers with one of the best returns on investment of the entire season. Ferguson was the clear-cut second read for Dak Prescott last year and will look to retain his place within the hierarchy in Dallas, thanks to very few off-season personnel changes. The Cowboys had the eighth most passing attempts in the league last year (614), leaving little room for additional statistical improvement for Ferguson. His weekly floor of nearly double-digit points in PPR leagues makes him a low-end TE1 in standard-size leagues.

2. **Dallas Goedert, PHI:** With six seasons of remarkedly consistent data to draw from, fantasy managers have a good idea of what to expect from Goedert entering 2024. Since 2019 (removing his rookie year as he was eased into the offense), Goedert has averaged 55 receptions, 650 receiving yards, and four touchdowns, usually finishing as a low-end TE1. He has endured his fair share of bumps and bruises and has unfortunately missed 14 games over the last four years. Surrounded by elite talent in Philadephia, the presence of A.J. Brown and DeVonta Smith limits his upside in the red zone, coupled with the Eagles' propensity to run quarterback sneaks around the goal line.

3. **T.J. Hockenson, DET:** The only reason that Hockenson dropped this far in our rankings is due to the gruesome knee injury that he suffered on Christmas Eve, where he tore his ACL and MCL. All reports have him on track with his rehab, but the expected timeline places his early-season availability in serious jeopardy, and he may miss the first month of the season. When fully healthy, Hockenson is a nightmare to cover over the middle of the field and a top-six tight end (as evidenced by his 95/960/5 split in 15 games before the injury). His prowess as a blocker results in few missed snaps, except the occasional necessary breather. Given the severity of the injury he is recovering from, fantasy managers should be mindful that he will likely be eased back into action and won't run his usual number of routes each week after being activated. Drafting Hockenson is an investment in the long game.

4. **Brock Bowers, LV:** One of the most dominant collegiate tight ends to emerge in the last 15 years, Bowers is the only player in history to be awarded the prestigious John Mackey award twice. A well-rounded player with a large 6'4, 230 lb. frame, Bowers's unique blend of size and athleticism makes him a significant mismatch for defenders downfield. During his three-year tenure at the University of Georgia, Bowers scored 31 touchdowns in 40 games despite constant double-teams. Head coach Antonio Pierce praised Bowers's versatility in the Raiders post-draft press conference, stating that "it is rare you can get a guy like him, who can line up as a slot receiver, work out of the backfield, catch reverses...". It is clear that Las Vegas intends to use him in any way it can to complement Davante Adams. We expect this rookie to make an immediate impact.

5. **Dalton Schultz, HOU:** Schultz finished 2023 with nearly identical numbers to his final season in Dallas and has become a reliable option for fantasy managers to draft after the first tier has passed. Finishing as the TE11 each of the last two seasons, Schultz inked a multi-year deal with Houston in the offseason and will provide young quarterback C.J. Stroud with another dependable set of hands in the receiving game. The Texans' decision to trade for Stefon Diggs in early April makes them favorites to retain the AFC South crown, but it bumps Schultz down to the fourth option in most passing situations, which is highly detrimental to any upside he once possessed. Schultz will continue to thrive down the seam when targeted and faces much less defensive attention compared to the options on the outside.

6. **Cole Kmet, CHI:** Kmet's fantasy outlook took dramatic swings amid the first round of the NFL draft, with Chicago selecting Caleb Williams and Rome Odunze. Williams represents a massive upgrade over Justin Fields as a passer and can provide catchable, accurate targets (a rarity under Fields) no matter what play is called. Unfortunately, Rome Odunze will provide Kmet with yet more opposition for looks in what was already an uphill battle against D.J. Moore and Keenan Allen. Fresh off his best season in the league (73/719/6), Kmet must find a way to carve out his own niche within the offense. Fantasy managers should draft him as a TE2 with modest upside.

7. **Pat Freiermuth, PIT:** Freiermuth finished as the TE12 in both 2021 and 2022 before falling off a cliff last year (along with the rest of the Steelers offense) and tumbling down to TE29, largely in part due to his lengthy IR stint because of an injured hamstring. A carousel of dreadful quarterbacks, the revitalization of George Pickens in the Pittsburgh offense, and the emergence of Jaylen Warren as a receiving threat out of the backfield severely diminished Freiermuth's target share. With Kenny Pickett and Diontae Johnson moving on to greener pastures, Freiermuth can quickly become an outlet for Russell Wilson as he acclimates himself into the offense. Though Freiermuth is the unquestioned starter at tight end atop the Steelers depth chart, we question his ability to overcome an extremely run-heavy offense now led by Arthur Smith. Draft him as a low-end TE1 with marginal upside.

Red Flags

1. **Luke Musgrave, GB:** Musgrave flashed several times early in the year for Green Bay, showing glimpses of why the Packers selected him in the second round from Oregon State. Unfortunately for his development, Musgrave was forced to miss six games in the middle of 2023 with a lacerated kidney, and fellow rookie Tucker Kraft played well in his absence. Before the injury, Musgrave averaged over seven points weekly in a PPR format and was a viable streaming option in deeper formats. For Musgrave to truly break out, he must separate himself from Kraft and the bevy of receivers that Jordan Love has at his disposal. An astounding ten players saw more than 24 targets for this team last year – that will need to condense drastically for Musgrave to have TE1 relevance.

2. **Hunter Henry, NE:** Much to the surprise of the fantasy community, Henry emerged as the overall TE1 through the first two weeks of the regular season and looked to be on his way to an actual breakout campaign. That bubble burst after Week 5 against New Orleans; from then on, he averaged less than four targets per game. Horrific quarterback play from Mac Jones and Bailey Zappe made it difficult for anyone on New England's roster to perform well, as the team finished with the fourth-fewest passing yards in the league and the sixth-fewest receiving touchdowns. Deciding to hit the refresh button, New England brought back Jacoby Brissett and drafted Drake Maye with the third-overall selection in the draft. Brissett is expected to start the season, while New England allows Maye to have a redshirt year. Brissett's hesitancy to look downfield (he has a career 6.6 YPA since 2016) plays into Henry's strength. He could have sneaky value in PPR formats, even with a low number of touchdown receptions.

3. **Juwan Johnson, NO:** A popular sleeper selection at the tight end position before last season's fantasy drafts, Johnson failed to live up to the hype and regressed in every relevant metric. A calf strain suffered during pregame warmups in Week 4 kept him off the field for four weeks, and he seemed unable to exhibit his usual explosive burst upon initially returning. He finally shook off the cobwebs in Week 15 and proceeded to catch a touchdown pass in three consecutive games to end the season. The departure of Michael Thomas in the offseason opens up additional targets for Johnson, who will look to return to his 2022 numbers when he finished as the TE8 with a 42/508/7 split.

4. **Cade Otton, TB:** Otton is entering his third season with Tampa Bay and has proven to be a solid, somewhat uninspiring, mid-range TE2 for fantasy. Mike Evans remains the dominant alpha in the Buccaneers offense and the top red-zone threat for Baker Mayfield to target. Instead, Otton competes for looks with Trey Palmer and Rachaad White on shorter routes closer to the line of scrimmage. Throughout an entire season in 2023, he averaged under 27 yards per game and a total of 67 targets, which placed him 21st amongst tight ends. His lack of upside and low volume on an offense that ranked 18th in passing yards and 10th in passing touchdowns last year relegates him to being a bye-week streaming option unless multiple injuries occur.

5. **Chigoziem Okonkwo, TEN:** After catching glimpses of his upside during his rookie 2022 campaign, fantasy managers were hopeful that Okonkwo would break out last year. A rise in snaps did result in a sharp uptick in targets (his 77 ranked second on the Titans), but he was held to just one touchdown reception and averaged under 10 YPC. Fortunately, Tennessee made many improvements in the offseason by solidifying their offensive line and bringing in additional weapons for Will Levis. The additions of Calvin Ridley and Tyler Boyd will ease defensive attention on Okonkwo, but his place in the pecking order for targets will undoubtedly fall. Given his expected ADP, Okonkwo makes an exciting dart throw as a TE2 with a monumental upside. Expect the Titans to transition into a more balanced offense after trading Derrick Henry to Baltimore.

6. **Tucker Kraft, GB:** Kraft is a player who would benefit from a change of scenery to demonstrate his true potential. Currently playing second-fiddle to Luke Musgrave, Kraft tantalized fantasy managers by showing them what he could do in Weeks 14-17 last year when he averaged over 10 points in PPR formats. Kraft is dealing with competition from Musgrave and faces an uphill battle against several capable receivers in Green Bay. Like Kraft, Romeo Doubs, Christian Watson, Dontayvion Wicks, and Bo Melton have demonstrated that they deserve looks from Jordan Love, significantly capping any upside that he possesses. Musgrave missing any significant portion of time would propel Kraft into high-end TE2 territory, but for now, we'd recommend adding him to your "player to watch" list and monitoring the situation.

7. **Isaiah Likely, BAL:** Likely is in a similar situation to Kraft, mentioned above. Any potential upside that Likely has is directly tied to the health of the incumbent start, in this case, Mark Andrews. Andrews has a unique connection with quarterback Lamar Jackson that is difficult to replicate, especially as a red zone threat. When Andrews missed time in 2023, Likely averaged nearly 14 points per week, including three games with 18 or more. When Andrews returned to the field, that number plummeted to under two in each contest. For fantasy purposes, he can be selected in deeper formats as a handcuff/insurance policy for Andrews, with the understanding that he carries little standalone value.

8. **Tyler Conklin, NYJ:** Conklin was one of the biggest winners of the most recent draft, thanks to the Jets opting to select Penn State tackle Olu Fashanu rather than the commonly-mocked Brock Bowers. New York's significant investments along the offensive line will hopefully pay dividends by keeping Aaron Rodgers upright – they can't afford to allow the amount of pressure they did last year. Conklin provides Rodgers with a sure set of hands capable of moving the chains, complementing the deep-play abilities of Garrett Wilson and Mike Williams. Fantasy managers looking to take a flier at the tight end position within the final few rounds of their drafts should keep an eye on Conklin, who will be a crucial contributor in a very high-powered New York offense.

9. **Noah Fant, SEA:** At first glance, Fant has all the traits one would hope for in a stud tight end. He has the prototypical size (6'4, 249 lbs.) and speed, with solid hands and above-average blocking skills. His college tape from Iowa was other-worldly, and he produces when targets are sent his way. So, what is the root cause for his struggles? A lack of consistent volume and the presence of another entrenched red zone threat. Seattle had a very uncharacteristic offensive scheme last year that should have led to Fant having a breakout with the second-fewest rushing attempts in the league. Oddly enough, they finished just 17th in passing attempts and 20th in receiving touchdowns – numbers indicating that the team was simply subpar. Fant's upside in fantasy hinges upon new offensive coordinator Ryan Grubb recognizing his talent and not letting it go to waste.

Chapter 8

Defense/Special Team

Scott Bogman

Although I prefer IDP, team defenses are probably what your league will stick with. Standard 12-team leagues with low-scoring defenses make the strategy easy. We pick on bad offenses, and only a few team defenses will emerge at the top, but that doesn't mean they should be blindly started. Last season, the Cowboys were the top-scoring team defense, and when we take a look at the game logs, we see they scored 10+ points in 8 weeks and fewer than 5 points 7 times. The Cowboys averaged fewer than 3 PPG in the three playoff weeks! Matchup is key. The Patriots were the lowest-scoring offense last season, and the 11.1 PPG they gave up to Defenses on average is a little better than the 10.5 the top-scoring Cowboys defense averaged. Pick on offenses that have been struggling, have injuries, or are on short rest, and you should find success!

Easy Early Season Schedule
Pittsburgh - @ ATL, @ DEN, vs LAC, @ IND
Cincinnati - vs NE, @ KC, vs WAS, @ CAR
Houston - @ IND, vs CHI, @ MIN, vs JAX
LA Chargers - vs LV, @ CAR, @ PIT, vs KC
Cleveland - vs DAL, @ JAX, vs NYG, @ LV
NY Jets - @ SF, @ TEN, vs NE, vs DEN

There are a few tough matchups in this group, but it's mainly filled with DEN, NE, WAS, and others that are adjusting to new offenses, new quarterbacks, or struggled last season.

Top 12 Defenses regardless of Matchup

1. Dallas Cowboys
2. New York Jets
3. Baltimore Ravens
4. Baltimore Ravens
5. San Francisco 49ers
6. Buffalo Bills
7. Pittsburgh Steelers
8. Kansas City Chiefs
9. Cleveland Browns
10. New Orleans Saints
11. Indianapolis Colts
12. Las Vegas Raiders

(In alphabetical order)

Arizona Cardinals - 3.8 FPPG (31st)
Up or down? There's nowhere to go but up! The Cards added help on the Defensive Line and the secondary through Free Agency and the draft. The improved run defense should help the defense get off the field quicker and give up fewer points.

Atlanta Falcons - 5.6 FPPG (28th)
Up or down? With coaching changes in Raheem Morris and Jimmy Lake coming over from the Rams to hit the reset button on the whole defense, it would be hard to see them downgrade. The Falcons also spent 5 of 8 picks on the defensive side of the ball, all in the front 7. Atlanta also gets back Andersen to start the season and Grady Jarrett at some point early. Making no significant changes in the secondary, changing the defensive calls, and an influx of youth could cause some growing pains early on, but there's room for growth here.

Baltimore Ravens - 10.2 FPPG (2nd)
Up or down? There isn't much room for growth here, but adding held to the only real weak spot in the draft (CB - Wiggins, Tampa) could make this defense even better. I don't think they'll get worse, which is why I still have them ranked 2nd. Patrick Queen was a significant loss, but they made a plan for him by drafting Trenton Simpson last year. Maybe Madubuike regresses, and the expected improvement from the secondary doesn't come to fruition. I don't expect there to be a big drop.

Buffalo Bills - 9.4 FPPG (3rd)
Up or down? Again, after finishing so high last season, it's hard to imagine the Bills improving. They added talent at each position in the draft, so it's not out of the realm of possibilities, but it would be surprising as Buffalo lost a lot of experience along the defensive line. I love Cole Bishop, the safety from Utah they took in the second round, but the combo of a rookie, Taylor Rapp, and Mike Edwards replacing Poyer and Hyde at S is likely to be a downgrade. I would say a little bit of a dip is to be expected, but they are still outstanding.

Carolina Panthers - 4.2 FPPG (30th)
Up or down? The Panthers traded their best defensive player, Brian Burns, but added talent through Free Agency and the draft. I would say they can't get worse, but losing not only Burns but also Donte Jackson, Frankie Luvu, Vonn Bell, and Jeremy Chinn might keep them in the basement for fantasy again.

Chicago Bears - 7.1 FPPG (t-17th)
Up or down? Bills DL coach Eric Washington is taking over the defense. He didn't make sweeping personnel changes and is trusting the talent here. An entire season of Montez Sweat, the addition of Kevin Byard at S, and the secondary gaining experience should improve the defense. I will say, for a defense in the middle of the pack, the Bears only spent one draft pick on defense in Edge rusher Austin Booker, which was surprising. I would have liked to have seen some upgrades on the IDL as well. The lack of upgrading for depth and a new play-caller could make things challenging, but I expect improvements.

Cincinnati Bengals - 6.9 FPPG (t-19th)
Up or down? Cincy couldn't stop anything last season, giving up the 5th most passing yards and the 7th most rushing yards. Cincy spent on Rankins to replace Reader and took Kris Jenkins and McKinnley Jackson in the draft to help stop the run. Cincy added back Vonn Bell through free agency, and Geno Stone came in to help replace the Safties in the porous secondary. Depending on D.J. Turner to take a jump at CB after a tough rookie season is asking a lot. I prefer the depth the Bengals have now, but Reader was a top 10 IDL in PFF RunD grade last season for a bad run D. I still expect improvements, but it's not hard to paint a picture where the Bengals are worse on defense in 24.

Cleveland Browns - 9 FPPG (5th)
Up or down? The prominent DL Free Agents in Za'Darius Smith and Shelby Harris came back, Jordan Hicks was added to improve the LB core, and the entire starting secondary came back. Mike Hall Jr in the 2nd was a substantial addition, and I think they stick in the Top 10.

Dallas Cowboys - 10.5 FPPG (1st)
Up or down? Matching a #1 Overall scoring season is tough, especially when the DC has moved on to greener pastures. Kendricks is an upgrade over LVE at LB, Diggs should be back, and adding talent at every spot outside of S in the draft should keep them high in PPG. There's not a lot of wiggle room, so they will probably move down, but I expect them to at least compete to be #1 again.

Denver Broncos - 6.9 FPPG (t-19th)
Up or down? I like the rookies they drafted in Jonah Ellis and Kris Abrams-Draine, but I'm not sure if Barton replacing Jewell or Franklin-Myers coming in are enough to improve on 2023 significantly. The offense getting better might be the best for this defense. I still think they'll get better, but not by enough to matter in most drafts. Surtain seemed to be on the trading block, and trading him would take the best player off the field on either side of the ball, so hopefully, he stays.

Detroit Lions - .6.3 FPPG (25th)
Up or down? The Lions couldn't stop the pass last season, so they traded for Carlton Davis, moved up in the 1st round for Terrion Arnold, and drafted Ennis Rakestraw in the 2nd round. The Lions also signed Marcus Davenport to help improve the pass rush and DJ Reader to help against the run. It's hard to see this defense not getting better.

Green Bay Packers - 6.8 FPPG (21st)
Up or down?: This team has sealed the leaks on defense. Edgerrin Cooper, Xavier McKinney, and Javon Bullard are new starters who add talent to an already good defense. The most significant change is letting Joe Barry walk and bringing in Jeff Hafley. This defense is on the verge of becoming dangerous. The only thing that would stop them would be more injuries to the CBs and no improvements from the young pass rushers.

Houston Texans - 7.7 FPPG (t-14th)
Up or down? The additions of Danielle Hunter, Denico Autry, Azeez Al-Shaair, and Kamari Lassiter can get the Texans closer to a Top 10 Fantasy Defense. I still have worries about the depth, so I haven't put them at a DST1 yet, but they are close. Anderson and Hunter have a chance to be one of the best pass-rushing duos in the league.

Indianapolis Colts - 8.2 FPPG (11th)
Up or down? Indy was way better than I thought last season, and there are still holes, but adding Latu in the draft should help the entire line. I still think the Colts need a new starting CB on the perimeter, but the LBs and DL are so strong that I feel the defense will be right on the DST 1-2 border most of the season.

Jacksonville Jaguars - 7.1 FPPG (t-17th)
Up or down? I don't think the Jags did enough in personnel to justify them any higher than a second-tier DST. Josh Allen coming back was enormous, but Travon Walker hasn't lived up to his draft spot. The secondary isn't any better than it was last season, in my opinion, and the LBs are exactly the same. New DC Ryan Neilsen is the key to unlocking the talent.

Kansas City Chiefs - 7.9 FPPG (12th)
Up or down? Losing Sneed is tough, but the main offseason goal was to get Chris Jones back, and they did. The Chiefs' defense was the strength of the team last season, and with the big man back in the middle, we are going to see another solid season. The offense putting up epic numbers again could boost them even more by allowing the line to get after the QB and the secondary to make plays late.

Las Vegas Raiders - 8.6 FPPG (7th)
Up or down? I really don't like that the Raiders didn't improve any of the starting secondary players, but adding Christian Wilkins to an already good line more than makes up for it. The Raiders are also moving Tyree Wilson inside, where he's better suited, and this might be the best defensive line in the league. The secondary makes the range of outcomes bigger but I'm a buyer on this defense.

Los Angeles Chargers - 6.6 FPPG (22nd)
Up or down? Jim Harbaugh and Jesse Minter will reshape this entire defense, and I expect it to happen fairly quickly. The IDL and LB will be where it starts with big personnel changes, and hopefully, the coaches can pull the talent out of the high-priced players on this defense. The growing pains will probably keep them low to start, but watch for this defense to come together quickly in the season and show signs of improvement.

Los Angeles Rams - 4.9 FPPG (29th)
Up or down? Being so low in scoring should mean we see an improvement, but the Rams lost their best player, Aaron Donald, who retired, and DC Raheem Morris left to become the Falcons' head coach. Verse, Fiske, Kinchens, Curl, White, and Davis will at least move the defense in the right direction.

Miami Dolphins - 8.9 FPPG (6th)
Up or down? I have concerns about the Dolphins defense stepping into 2024. The main issue I see is that Jaelan Phillips and Bradley Chubb are likely to start the season on the PUP. Phillips has said he expects to be back Week 1, but coming off a torn Achilles, I doubt it very much. Drafting Chop Robinson and signing Shaq Barrett are nice moves, but replacing the starting Edge Rushers, the play-calling LB, and some pieces in the secondary have me worried about repeatability for a strong defense from last season. Hopefully, the new DC Anthony Weaver will have some tricks up his sleeve!

Minnesota Vikings - 7.3 FPPG (16th)
Up or down? I think the player movement will be good overall for the Vikings. Losing one of the best edge rushers in Danielle Hunter stings, but Greenard was a great signing, and Dallas Turner can develop into a beast at Edge. Hicks to Cashman is lateral at LB, but I like Grugier-Hill going to the highest blitzing rate team in the NFL, and I would bet on a slight improvement overall.

New England Patriots - 6.4 FPPG (t-23rd)
Up or down? Well, the best thing for this defense would be the offense holding the ball a little more. The Pats were 31st in Time of Possession last season and even with a strong defense will falter under those conditions. The Pats defense played at a Top 10 level after their bye week. They will get back key pieces like Matthew Judon and Christian Gonzalez and I expect the offense to improve to make them at least a matchup play.

New Orleans Saints - 8.5 FPPG (t-8th)
Up or down? This defense was already strong, and the Saints added some nice pieces in Chase Young to the DL, Willie Gay at LB, and rookie Kool-Aid McKinstry at CB. The Saints schedule looks particularly nice after Week 5 when they get Dallas, Philly, and Kansas City behind them to enter a stretch of TB, DEN, LAC, CAR, ATL, and CLE.

New York Giants - 7.7 FPPG (t-14th)
Up or down? The addition of Brian Burns has a chance to make this one of the most formidable defensive lines in the league. Dexter Lawrence is now the best IDL in the NFL since Aaron Donald retired, and young pass rushers Ojulari and Thibodeaux should get more opportunities. The secondary is still dicey, but it will go a long way if the young core can play a little better. It'll probably be a bit of high highs with low lows, but I would have them right around the same range as 2023 because they overperformed a touch for fantasy.

New York Jets - 9.1 FPPG (4th)
Up or down? An already Top-5 defense moving up is a big ask, but I think the Jets are the team to do it! The offense is going to be WAY better with Aaron Rodgers; they added Haason Reddick at Edge and only really lost S Jordan Whitehead and he was replaced by a vet in Chuck Clark. The Jets are poised to be even better, and I'm a big believer!

Philadelphia Eagles - 5.9 FPPG (27th)
Up or down? The Eagles defense was ROUGH last season as they gave up the 2nd most passing yards in the NFL. However, the problem has been addressed with enthusiasm! The Eagles signed Gardner-Johnson back and spent 1st AND 2nd round picks on CBs in Quinyon Mitchell and Cooper DeJean. The Eagles also signed LB Devin White, signed Edge Bryce Huff, and spent a 3rd round pick on Edge Jalyx Hunt. I expect a return to big-time production for Philly!

Pittsburgh Steelers - 8.4 FPPG (t-8th)
Up or down? Pittsburgh's defensive roster is a little better than last season, but there are still holes in the secondary. The defensive line is still one of the best in the league with Watt and Highsmith and, the LBs have better starters and depth. However, the starting Slot CB is in the air, and the safety position is still weak outside of Minkah. I think their still Top-10 but are probably it won't be flawless.

San Francisco 49ers - 8.3 FPPG (10th)
Up or down? The 9ers are in a similar situation as Pittsburgh. I think they are better now by getting Hufanga back from injury, improving the secondary depth, and adding Edge depth. The issue is that the LBs are still thin with Greenlaw down, and the IDL took a step back when they lost Kinlaw and Ferrell. Three different defensive coordinators in the last three seasons may mean growing pains. The roster moves make them about the same as last season, which is a very strong defense that will have a lot of points in fantasy.

Seattle Seahawks - 6.4 FPPG (t-23rd)
Up or down? The Seahawks made a lot of moves, but I don't know if they all add up to a significant improvement. The defensive line was improved by drafting IDL Byron Murphy in the 1st, resigning Leonard Williams, and Uchenna Nwosu returning from his torn pec. The LBs are probably lateral, going from Wagner and Brooks to Baker and Dodson, but there is way less experience there now. The CBs are young and improving, but I really don't like going from Diggs to Jenkins at S. The DL is good enough to improve them as a whole, but an immediate improvement is asking a lot, especially with a new defensive coaching staff.

Tampa Bay Buccaneers - 7.8 FPPG (13th)
Up or down? This is one of the few defenses I'm confident will take a bit of a step back. The Bucs let Devin White and Shaq Barrett walk, traded Carlton Davis, and only brought in aging vet Randy Gregory and one starter in S Jordan Whitehead. Players like McCollum, Tykee Smith, and Chris Braswell will have to catch fire quickly to improve this defense from the jump. I think a slight step back is the most reasonable outcome.

Tennessee Titans - 6 FPPG (26th)
Up or down? Tennessee HAS to get better on defense with all of the coaching changes and personnel upgrades they made. Sweat, Murray, Awuzie, AND Sneed all represent upgrades from last season. They added depth at LB and the only position that didn't get a boost was Saftey. Jeffery Simmons health will be the biggest determining factor but I haven't seen any setbacks in his recovery from a knee injury.

Washington Commanders - 3.8 FPPG (t-31st)
Up or down? This one is easy because the Commanders have nowhere to go but up! Dan Quinn is coming over from Dallas, and wholesale changes have been made with seven new starters coming over in free agency or the draft. Washington should be able to sustain some injuries as well, with improved depth at every position. Armstrong, Ferrell, Wagner, Luvu, Newton, Chinn, Davis, and Sainristil might not make Washington great, but they will make them better at the very least!

Chapter 9

IDP: Individual Defensive Players

Scott Bogman

I usually use this part of the Black Book to preach about IDP and use this as a sales pitch for people to play it. I won't do that again. I'll just say that I have been playing IDP since the late 1900s. I've been creating content for IDP for over ten years, and I have never once had someone tell me they played and didn't enjoy it. I enjoy both sides of the ball, and I really don't like taking team defenses and losing because the same CB keeps getting torched or the Interior Defensive Lineman can't stop the run. I want to be able to control that side of the ball and add value by picking the right players.

There are different types of scoring in IDP, so be sure to pay attention to how the IDPs score and how much they score compared to the offensive positions. One of the questions I get most often is when to start drafting IDPs in redraft, and the answer always depends on how much they score. In general, the top IDPs will score in the neighborhood of an RB/WR3, so the top IDPs go in the 7th/8th round, and they really start coming off the board past round 10. The Scoring system I rank for is tackle-heavy instead of big play-heavy. Adjust accordingly if your league gives out bonuses for TO yardage or awards a lot of points for big plays.

DEFENSIVE LINEMEN

The DL is the most rotated position in the NFL. Only two DLs (Crosby and Hunter) played over 1000 snaps last season, while 16 LBs and 33 DBs did. This makes the DL less trustworthy for points and much shallower. I like to get an early DL or a big-time LB to start, and I would really prefer two of my top 12 DLs if I have to start at least two. LBs are deeper, and DBs are WAY deeper. It doesn't work out for every tier but the DL1s are really a tier of their own. I would mix DL2 with a lot of DL3, and there are a lot of rookies that could develop quickly. DL is a little more forgiving this season but still remains the least reliable IDP position.

DL1
Maxx Crosby, Myles Garrett, Danielle Hunter, Josh Allen, Aidan Hutchinson, Brian Burns, Alex Highsmith, Will Anderson Jr., Montez Sweat, Jonathan Greenard, Trey Hendrickson, Nick Bosa

DL2
Christian Wilkins, Derrick Brown, DeForest Buckner, Carl Granderson, Jon Cooper, Jermaine Johnson, Zach Sieler, Kayvon Thibodeaux, George Karlaftis, Boye Mafe, Ed Oliver, Christian Barmore

DL3
Demarcus Lawrence, Michael Hoecht, Jeffery Simmons, Malcolm Koonce, Sam Hubbard, Quinnen Williams, Kwity Paye, Gregory Rousseau, D.J. Wonnum, Jadeveon Clowney, Travon Walker, Justin Madubuike, Chris Jones

LINEBACKERS

The LB position plays out, in the depth of the position, similar to QBs in that the best players don't come off the field, and when they are replaced, the production doesn't always match up. Scoring-wise, the LBs play like WRs, meaning it's an arms race because there is a lot of depth, and the more LBs you are allowed to play, the more critical the depth becomes. I have a lot of trust through the first two LB groups and there's a lot of upside plays all the way through.

LB1
Foye Oluokun, Zaire Franklin, Bobby Wagner, Roquan Smith, Fred Warner, T.J. Watt, Bobby Okereke, Ernest Jones, Terrel Bernard, C.J. Mosley, Patrick Queen, Robert Spillane

LB2
Quincy Williams, Micah Parsons, Lavonte David, T.J. Edwards, Alex Singleton, Logan Wilson, Tremaine Edmunds, Quay Walker, Nick Bolton, Josey Jewell, Jordan Hicks, Frankie Luvu

LB3
Azeez Al-Shaair, Eric Kendricks, Devin White, Kyzir White, Troy Andersen, Kenneth Murray, Jordyn Brooks, Devin Lloyd, Edgerrin Cooper, Kaden Elliss, Blake Cashman, Alex Anzalone

LB4
Ja'Whaun Bentley, Jeremiah Owusu-Koramoah, Christian Harris, Jerome Baker, Ivan Pace, Demario Davis, Micah McFadden, E.J. Speed, Willie Gay, Germaine Pratt, Tyrel Dodson, Divine Deablo

DEFENSIVE BACKS

DB has been and always will be the deepest position in IDP, and it's the deepest in Fantasy. We want high-tackle-total Safties first, with some CBs sprinkled in. The CBs have to be on the field a lot and should be somewhere around league average, so they actually get thrown at but stay on the field. The 'Rookie CB Rule' has the young CBs being targeted, last season, both Devon Witherspoon and Tyrique Stevenson were inside the top 5 in PPG among CBs. DBs should be last to be drafted and first to be cut when they don't perform because there will be options on the wire in even VERY deep leagues.

DB1
Antoine Winfield, Kyle Hamilton, Derwin James, Jaquan Brisker, Jessie Bates, Xavier McKinney, Julian Love, Minkah Fitzpatrick, Kyle Dugger, Buddha Baker, Brian Branch, Kamren Curl

DB2
Julian Blackmon, Kevin Byard, Kenny Moore, Devon Witherspoon, Nate Hobbs, Josh Metellus, Jevon Holland, Jalen Pitre, Reed Blankenship, Camryn Bynum, Justin Reid, Jalen Thompson

DB3
Grant Delpit, Jordan Poyer, Donovan Wilson, Tyler Nubin, Jordan Whitehead, Kerby Joseph, Alohi Gilman, Tyrique Stevenson, Trent McDuffie, Paulson Adebo, Harrison Smith, Jabrill Peppers

Chapter 10

Kickers

2024 Ranks

RK	TIERS	PLAYER NAME	RK	TIERS	PLAYER NAME
1	1	Brandon Aubrey	8	2	Jake Moody
2	1	Justin Tucker	9	2	Younghoe Koo
3	1	Jason Sanders	10	3	Evan McPherson
4	2	Ka'imi Fairbairn	11	3	Dustin Hopkins
5	2	Harrison Butker	12	3	Cairo Santos
6	2	Jake Elliott	13	3	Matt Gay
7	2	Tyler Bass	14	3	Cameron Dicker

I highly recommend NOT playing fantasy football with kickers. They are a pain when it comes to roster space, and their scoring can be arbitrary on a weekly basis. As you can see, there really isn't much of a difference between them in scoring for the top 12.

Player	'23 FPTS/G	Player	'23 FPTS/G
1 Brandon Aubrey (DAL)	10.6	8 Blake Grupe (NO)	8.8
2 Dustin Hopkins (CLE)	9.9	9 Brandon McManus (WAS)	8.6
3 Cairo Santos (CHI)	9.3	10 Jason Sanders (MIA)	8.6
4 Matt Gay (IND)	9.2	11 Evan McPherson (CIN)	8.2
5 Jake Elliott (PHI)	9.2	12 Chase McLaughlin (TB)	8
6 Harrison Butker (KC)	9.1	13 Chris Boswell (PIT)	7.8
7 Cameron Dicker (LAC)	8.9	14 Matt Prater (ARI)	7.6

Less than 3 points on average separate K1 from K14 in 2023, and only 2 points from K1 to K10 in a shallow 10-person league. So, reaching for an advantage in any normal scoring is a bad idea. Now, some leagues have wacky scoring, and if, for some reason, kickers make a larger impact, then you can consider that in your draft strategy. I would also advise against playing in that scoring format.

If you insist on having kickers in your league, follow a few guidelines when selecting a kicker:

- Good offenses
- Late bye weeks
- Home schedules with domes or good climates

And please, wait until the absolute last round to select one, as they are more interchangeable than you realize, and even going a round before your final round could cost you this year's De'Von Achane or Rashee Rice. Both were last-round or undrafted in most leagues. Take fliers on these young upside players instead of what you envision as the "best kicker."

Chapter 11

Dynasty Strategy
Scott Bogman

Dynasty is absolutely my favorite version of Fantasy Football! The challenge is more complex as one mistake can cost you a player who is good for years, but the sword cuts both ways, and the good decisions carry your squad.

Dynasty can seem intimidating for starters, but it can be played in many ways. Traditional Dynasty involves keeping all your players with no limits. 'Keeper' leagues allow a certain number of players or a defined time frame to keep players. I have also seen leagues that play for 3, 5, or more years and the whole league resets. Another popular version involves increasing the number of players kept; start with three and add one every year. If you are looking for more complicated leagues, I've done them down the line with salary caps, free agency, and all of the bells and whistles one could imagine. Currently, the most complicated league I play in is 32 teams with doubles of every player (no, you can't roster the same player twice), with IDPs.

My tiers represent a keep-forever league, but my mindset is a 3+ year window. I have noticed that older players who can still contribute get passed. I take advantage of that in the initial draft, finishing high in the first few seasons and trying to let the league pay for itself and build from there. I usually lean towards the younger player when drafting from the same tier. Some like to "tank" the first few seasons and set themselves up for longer-term success, while others try to play the balancing act and have it all. I have seen every type of strategy work, and I've also seen them all crash and burn, so there isn't a 'magical' winning formula. If you prefer a longer-term build, focus on the younger players from each tier, and if you want to win sooner, stick closer to a redraft list.

QUARTERBACKS

The quarterback position received an influx of talent this season, with six players being drafted in the first round and five expected to become starters by at least the end of the season! My tiers are probably a little deeper than most because I'm looking at the aforementioned '3+ years window'. 1 QB leagues have already been easy to draft QB for, but even SF leagues are pretty deep now, with 27 of my top 30 going into the season as starters (Fields/Penix Jr./Howell start on the bench). Some of the QBs I'll call 'conditional' may be as early as Burrow with his injury history or Stroud with only one year of success so far, but others are for age, injuries, or needing to 'prove it' this year to keep the job moving forward. Anyone beyond Tier 4 I consider a longshot to hold much value beyond this season and should be handcuffs or bench options only.

Tier 1 - Studs now and beyond
Josh Allen, Lamar Jackson, Patrick Mahomes, Jalen Hurts, C.J. Stroud, Joe Burrow

These are the guys that I feel can be QB1 for the upcoming season and the next 3-5 years. We have the rushing upside from Allen, Jackson, and Hurts. The rushing injury risk is considered in the ranking. Stroud being a 1-year sensation, and Burrow's recent injury history are the 'risky' picks for Tier 1.

Burrow missed time, but he finished as QB4 in 22, and the Bengals added talent to the OL, franchised Higgins, and gave him some good TE targets. I'm confident that if he plays the

Stroud doesn't have the rushing upside, but he did run for 3 TDs, win ROY, and had the lowest INT total among starting QBs last season. The Texans also traded for Diggs, got a healthy Tank Dell back, AND added Joe Mixon. I think we see a rookie-to-2nd-year leap for Stroud and that he belongs here.

Tier 2 - Potential QB1
Caleb Williams, Anthony Richardson, Jayden Daniels, J.J. McCarthy, Justin Herbert, Trevor Lawrence

This Tier is the guys that can make 'the leap' into the next tier as soon as this season if everything goes right. Caleb Williams is as close to 'a sure thing' as they come, and the Bears added Keenan Allen and 1st round pick Rome Odunze to the arsenal. Rookies Jayden Daniels and J.J. McCarthy also ended up in favorable situations to start their careers. Daniels will be in Kliff Kingsbury's offense, which made Kyler Murray so valuable, and McCarthy goes to the Vikings' pass-heavy offense with Jefferson and Addison to start his career. Richardson, we only saw a taste of last season with three starts. Still, he was one of the top 10 quarterbacks in PPG in that showing. The Colts added a weapon in 2nd round pick Adonai Mitchell to pair with Pittman and Taylor, and too many good receiving TE options have this offense moving into scary territory quickly.

Justin Herbert would be in the top tier if he had Kingsbury or O'Connell calling the shots, but Harbaugh's preference to run the ball and hiring Greg Roman makes me wary of Herbert's ceiling moving forward. Herbert has a rushing upside that may have been forgotten, but I think he may not be asked to run enough after the rib injury last season to make it a stable asset. Trevor Lawrence is on the fence, and it's not all his fault for the start he was given under Urban Meyer. Lawrence took a nice jump in his 2nd year but suffered multiple minor injuries last season and didn't grow in fantasy value. I expect Lawrence to jump into Tier 1 or fall to Tier 3 after this season.

Tier 3 - Still VERY good
Drake Maye, Kyle Murray, Dak Prescott, Jordan Love, Brock Purdy, Tua Tagovailoa

I had Drake Maye as my 2nd quarterback in this draft, and I think he will be a good quarterback, but landing in New England during a rebuilding of the offense is tough to start. The Patriots are likely to approach the QB position slowly, and we've already had the 'He has a lot to work on' quote from Jerod Mayo during rookie minicamp. Drake will start this year, but this will be a run-the-ball, play-strong defense approach as the Patriots rebuild the offense.

I might be low on Kyler. He has been an outstanding fantasy asset in his career, but most of that was under Kingsbury. Murray still was a QB1 in the eight games he started, and the Cardinals added Marvin Harrison Jr. in the draft. Still, this ranking is more about my fear that his rushing will be less reliable the deeper we get into his career, and he's already had one major injury.

Dak is one of the best in the NFL, and the Cowboys may rely on him even more this year without a viable bell-cow RB, but he's turning 31 this year, and the mileage is piling up. I'll err on the side of history and time when it comes to QBs over the age of 30, but the shorter the window you're working in, the more valuable Dak becomes.

Goff was on the border of this tier because I wasn't sure if the Lions were 100% committed to him. Goff's recent extension shows he's going to be running this powerful offense until 2027, at least.

Jordan Love was SO GOOD in his 1st season as a starter I just wonder a bit about repeatability. Love was so comfortable in the pocket, the Packers added Josh Jacobs and spent a pick on MarShawn Lloyd to possibly expand the run game, they run a slower pace are all factors that make me believe Love was close to his ceiling last year. Love is also a free agent after this season, which makes his future murky, but I expect him to get an extension before the season starts.

It's obvious that Brock Purdy is better than most thought, and he has the keys to an amazing offense. The 9ers added another weapon in Pearsall in the draft as well, BUT Purdy hasn't been extended yet. I expect a good season will earn him an extension, but a mediocre season could find San Francisco drafting his replacement or signing a free agent.

Speaking of free agents, Tua is still waiting on his. Tua is an exceptional QB in a great system for his skillset but he has no rushing upside and has a history of concussions which makes him a riskier investment or I'd have him right under Lawrence in the 2nd tier.

4th Tier - Have to play well to keep the job (or earn the job for the non-starters)
Bryce Young, Deshaun Watson, Justin Fields, Bo Nix, Kirk Cousins, Michael Penix. Jr., Matthew Stafford. Baker Mayfield, Will Levis. Daniel Jones, Sam Howell

This is the tier, mainly, the 'one year to keep your job' QBs. Penix Jr, Howell, and Nix are the outliers from the rest, and they should have a longer runway. Penix offers the most upside, but the likelihood is waiting at least a season and a half if Cousins doesn't turn into a pumpkin after his Achilles injury. Nix is getting the hype from his coach and could be their starter for a long time but the offense is likely to be designed around the run with so many good RBs on the roster and one of the weakest WR groups in the league. Howell isn't going into this season as a starter, but the Seahawks were very happy to get him and he's viewed as the eventual replacement for Geno. We saw Howell's wide range of results, so a year or two on the bench could help him in the long run.

I think it's early to give up on Young, but the NFL is unforgiving. If he struggles again, the Panthers pick high. If there's a quarterback good enough to be taken, they'll have to consider one, and they could look hard at a bridge veteran FA to compete. Dave Canales has been behind Geno Smith and Baker Mayfield for the past two seasons, so we'll see if he can fix Young. He's definitely better than what we saw last season.

Watson is going to get another year for the Browns, but they signed two quarterbacks, and Russell Wilson's getting cut has changed my perspective on the chances of that happening for Watson. Watson is also yet to look like the same guy he was in Houston and is coming off shoulder surgery, so my enthusiasm is close to dead.

Justin Fields has shown us that his upside is real, but the NFL has shown us that they don't think much of him at this point. Fields must take advantage of his next opportunity or risk fading into obscurity.

Will Levis is going to get a shot, but Callahan wasn't there when Levis was drafted, so he needs to perform well quickly to avoid being replaced by Mason Rudolph this year and someone else next year.

Daniel Jones didn't get replaced this year, but not because of a lack of trying by the Giants. Jones's contract isn't insurmountable if New York wants to cut him after this season so he's another QB that has a short window to keep his job.

5th Tier - Starters this year and good handcuffs
Derek Carr, Geno Smith, Aaron Rodgers, Gardner Mishew, Russell Wilson, Aidan O'Connell, Trey Lance, Spencer Rattler, Mac Jones, Kenny Pickett

The old men here have two years tops; Carr, Smith, and Wilson are watching the window close, and Rodgers is likely in his last season. Carr probably has two years left in New Orleans because of his contract, but Smith is with a new coach on a team that has already planned to replace him, and Wilson probably gets six weeks or less to prove he belongs before the Steelers move to Fields. Minshew is better than O'Connell, and he's the 'two-year plan' for the Raiders, but one bad streak, and they'll go right to O'Connell, I think. Lance is still an interesting option in SF because we still really haven't seen him enough to say he can't get the job done, and the Cowboys haven't extended Dak. I find Rattler interesting because I like the idea of a new coach coming into New Orleans next season and making the quarterback job an open competition between Rattler, Carr, and probably a draft pick or free agent. Pickett and Jones are 1st round picks who were put in bad situations to start their career, so the NFL is likely to be more forgiving and give them a few looks, and if an injury happens, they both will get to run offenses with way more weapons than they've had in the past.

Tier 6 - handcuffs and longshots
Hendon Hooker, Michael Pratt, Zach Wilson, Sam Darnold, Bailey Zappe, Tyler Huntley, Jake Browning, Desmond Ridder

Hooker, Pratt, and Browning are all here as QBs that are behind very good QBs but should something happen, they would hold a lot of value in SF leagues. Wilson, Darnold, and Ridder are all experienced enough to keep getting work as backups, and I think Zappe and Huntley will find themselves in this group as well. Huntley should be higher, but it seems like he's 3rd in Cleveland now.

Tier 7 - We've waited too long to take a QB
Jimmy Garoppolo, Jameis Winston, Jacoby Brissett, Joshua Dobbs, Tyson Bagent, Drew Lock, Carson Wentz, Jordan Travis, Mason Rudolph, Joe Milton, Malik Willis. Dorian Thompson-Robinson. Marcus Mariota, Joe Flacco, Kyle Trask

This is the group that I don't really see having a lot of value moving forward. There are upside plays in Bagent, Travis, Milton, Willis, Thompson-Robinson and Trask. In his games last season, Bagent was decent, but Caleb Williams's leash will be extremely long, so he's a handcuff moving forward. Travis could have a shot as early as next year with Rodgers and Taylor nearing the end of their careers, and fellow rookie Milton needs development and will be able to take advantage of holding a clipboard for a while. DTR and Willis are young enough to get another shot and maybe pick the offense they like. Brissett is the only one of the vets that looks like a lock for playing time, and the others are all handcuffs.

RUNNING BACKS

Running Backs have a shorter shelf life than the other positions, so various draft strategies are created. I'm designing my tiers to give options inside each for the different types of strategies that drafters may use. I would like to get one 'upper tier' RB if I can, get an older vet that falls a bit (like Henry or Kamara this year), and then take some youthful upside. RBs are way more limited than WRs in terms of sheer numbers, of course, BUT managers tend to trade them away cheaper in-season when the RB in question gets deeper in their career to avoid the 'cliff drop' at the end. The RBs get expensive in Rookie Drafts this year. I've seen Jonathon Brooks go over Brock Bowers in all 3 of my rookie drafts. I'm a Texas fan, and I love Brooks, but there are VERY few scenarios in which I would select him over Bowers. However, the positional need drives their price up during rookie drafts. I'm not suggesting taking Bowers if you have Kelce and LaPorta on your roster or anything crazy, but the short shelf life makes the values of RBs fluctuate from expensive in drafts to cheap in trades. The 2025 RB class looks rich with talent, so RBs with a shorter window might be a little more replaceable than in the past. The RB value has wilted as 30 touchbacks slip into oblivion, but there will always be some RBs that are impossible to take off the field because they are so much better than the other options. Whatever strategy you decide to utilize, there is an option in almost every tier I have here!

Tier 1 - Talent + Workload
Bijan Robinson, Breece Hall, Christian McCaffrey, Jonathan Taylor, Jahmyr Gibbs

CMC continues to be the best RB in the NFL by a decent margin, but he's turning 28 this year, and the drop-off for RBs is vast and sharp. CMC has been top 5 in PPG every year since 2018 and has had the highest RB point total in 3 of those seasons. His upside is higher than any other RB, but his expiration date is closer than that of the rest of this tier.

Bijan didn't put together the best rookie season we've seen by an RB, but the offense was completely inept, and he was still able to put up RB2 numbers despite that. This season, with Zac Robinson calling the plays, a vastly improved QB (even if Cousins isn't ready and they have to go with Penix), and what will likely be a more defined role, there's a much better chance that he hits his potential quickly. Breece Hall had an incredible season in a similar situation as Bijan, with more competent play calling, in my opinion. Robinson and Hall can benefit from more goal-line opportunities; Bijan had three carries and three targets inside the 5-yard line, and Hall only had 1 of each last season. I give Bijan the slightest of edges over Breece because the Rams offense (that new OC Robinson is coming from) gave Kyren 17 carries inside the 5, and he converted 9 for TDs.

Taylor has missed 13 games the past two seasons, so I completely understand if that makes him a player to avoid to some. My confidence in Taylor isn't so much that I think he'll magically return to being injury-free, but it's that all RBs get hit, especially the high-volume players, and carry a similar risk. I love what the Colts are building on offense, and we only saw Taylor and Richardson together for half a game last year. Taylor finished with 51 carries in Indy's last two games, so I think he'll be fine to start the season, and the fact they didn't add another RB in free agency or the draft shows me the Colts believe he'll be fine as well.

There's already a buzz about Gibbs. He was so good last season; the only thing missing was more touches. Gibbs had the 8th most PPR points last season with the 25th most touches, and GB Brad Holmes has already spoken about Gibbs getting more carries. I was a little concerned about TD repeatability with Gibbs, but if he gets more touches, it becomes way less of a concern, and repeatability is more realistic.

Tier 2 - 1st option on offense
Kenneth Walker III, Kyren Williams, Devon Achane, Saquon Barkley, Travis Etienne, James Cook, Josh Jacobs, Rachaad White

Walker is one of my favorite RBs to watch, probably ever. His dominance of Michigan during his final season in College was when Cupid's arrow struck me in the heart. Walker hasn't been higher than an RB1 yet, so this is a bit of a projection, but as I mentioned earlier, I think Macdonald and Grubb will run the ball behind the two good RBs, which would make Walker way more appealing. I'll admit there's a bit of risk in the 'ifs' for Walker *if* they pass the ball more than expected *if* Charbonnet gets more work, *if* he gets fewer carries inside the 5 are all real situations to cloud him, but he's so talented. Among these RBs, Walker was 2nd in missed tackles forced, and he was only behind him by 8 with 77 fewer touches; Walker was 2nd in Breakaway yards and elusive rating behind only Achane in those who had 118 fewer touches.

Kyren had the seventh-most PPR points despite playing only 12 games last season! TD repeatability could be an issue, of course, but he'll hopefully have five more games to make up the difference. Corum will impact his touches a bit, but Williams is much more accomplished in the run game.

Cook, Jacobs, and White are all getting a rookie RB thrown in the mix, but I expect more of the same from them. These three RBs are still young and the first option on offense, and even with some competition, I expect that to stay the same.

Etienne is in the same boat as these guys, except the Jags didn't draft someone this year. It seems they'll add to Bigsby's workload, but I don't expect anyone to challenge him once we get to the season. As long as he can handle it, he'll pace for another 300+ touches.

Achane is not a conventional running back; he'll never be a 25+ touch player in the NFL because he's undersized and missed time in his first season. Achane averaged the 5th most PPR points for RBs last season; he had 22 runs over 10 yards last season, which was 17th in the league despite having the 47th most carries, and he had a 54% Breakaway yardage percentage last season while the 2nd most among RBs with 100 carries was Hall (and he was the only other RB over 40% at 40.5). Achane could have a shorter career, but it also could last longer with limited touches. Give me the talent, even if it's hard to project.

Tier 3 - RB2 with upside
Isiah Pacheco, Rhamondre Stevenson, Tony Pollard, Najee Harris, Javonte Williams, Jonathan Brooks, Trey Benson, Derrick Henry, Alvin Kamara, Brian Robinson Jr., Joe Mixon

Pacheco, Rhamondre, Pollard, Najee, Javonte, King Henry, Kamara, and Mixon will all lead their teams in touches this year at the very least, but their future is a little murkier than the previous Tier. I might be a bit low on Pacheco even though it's only one spot in ECR, but the offense will always work through Mahomes. Stevenson missed time last year but will be back and wants to be back in his lead role. However, 41% of his production came from receiving, and I expect Antonio Gibson to take the majority of those duties, which caps his upside. I believe in Pollard, but he's on a 3-year deal that the Titans can get out easily in two years. Najee didn't have his 5th-year option picked up, but he's going to what looks to be the heaviest run game in the league this year and could easily earn another contract, making his upside high even if capped by Jaylen Warren. This is the proverbial 'make or break' year for Javonte, and there are so many ways he can go. My prediction is that he looks improved another year /removed from his ACL injury, and, he is the anchor of the offense with QB AND WR issues. Henry is still a beast, but he's 30. Kamara will be 29 before the season starts, but he finished as RB3 overall last season.

The 'Old Men' can easily be RB1s this season, but the stars burn out quickly at the end. Maybe we will get two years and a slower decline, or the next injury could slow them down for good. Conditional RBs are a dice roll, but I'm trying to win ASAP in most cases, and the upcoming RB class looks loaded.

Brian Robinson is interesting because the Kingsbury offense in Arizona produced an RB1 twice when James Conner was in town, but he never had an RB of Ekeler's caliber. Brian Robinson is an RB I love, but the situation makes me less confident in his total number of touches because Ekeler is just a year removed from being the #1 PPR RB.

The Rookies Brooks and Benson landed in good scenarios. Benson is behind James Conner for this season, but Conner will be a free agent after this season. Brooks is coming off an ACL injury in November, going into his rookie year, so there might be a portion of this season that he misses although the updates have been positive. The Panthers have invested in free agency and the draft to this offense, so we should at least see it move in the right direction. Brooks is a big part of that plan.

Tier 4 - The Goods - can be, used to be, will be
Zach Charbonnet, David Montgomery, Jaylen Wright, Nick Chubb, Austin Ekeler. D'Andre Swift, James Conner, Aaron Jones, Jaylen Warren, Blake Corum, Chase Brown, Jerome Ford, Zamir White

Charbonnet, Wright, Corum, and Warren are the RBs that are #2 backs going into this year. Charbonnet and Warren are getting new OCs that I think will benefit them. Charbonnet still has a lot to prove and is blocked, but the talent usually finds a way to make an impact. If the Steelers' plan of running downhill is successful, I could be low on Warren. Arthur Smith had the 6th most RB Targets last season, and Warren tied for 5th in targets. The fit seems nice, but I'm lower than consensus on Warren because I think he'll be limited in the maximum number of touches he'll have. I love the fit for Wright in Miami, although with Mostert playing so well, we might have to wait a bit to see it from Wright. Corum got a lot of Kyren Williams comps, and with the injuries Kyren had last season and the lack of options behind him, they made Corum a priority, which means he should have an immediate role and contribute from Day 1. Still, Kyren was RB2 in PPG last season, it will be hard to take the ball away from him.

Montgomery is in a weird spot because he was a high-end RB2 last year, and now we know he will cede touches to Gibbs, which means he's losing value this year and will be a cut candidate next season. Monty is a good RB, but his future is murky, which makes him more of a risk than I would like.

I would consider Ekeler a good 'bounce-back' candidate in a system that fits his skill set. As I mentioned before, he was RB1 Overall in 2022. I'm not a believer in Swift; I think his success last season was a lot from the Eagles OL. The Bears offense could make an enormous jump quickly here, and Swift is still the lead back, which holds a lot of value. Conner and Jones are lead backs who are both good enough to be high-end RB2s this year, but they are both free agents over 30 going into next season, which makes their future challenging to bank on.

The final trio of this tier, Brown, Ford, and White, are all backs who I expect to lead their teams in touches among RBs and have youth on their side. Brown and White are both taking over for the first time as the primary backs in their offenses. White got a taste of it at the end of last season, getting over 20 carries a piece in the last three games for the Raiders, and he put up some big numbers. It was nice to see White get the run because he only had over 20 carries twice in College. Carries aren't an issue for Chase Brown, as he had 30 or more carries in his final season at Illinois 5 times. Brown has to beat out veteran free agent Zack Moss to earn touches, but while Moss is a strong RB, he has also been plagued with injuries throughout his collegiate and pro career. Ford proved to me last season that he can take this job and be productive, but the Browns are going to see if Chubb can recover from this horrific knee injury first, which might cap Ford to start at least.

Tier 5 - Limited touches or time
Roschon Johnson, Tyler Allgeier, Raheem Mostert, Ray Davis, MarShawn Lloyd, Tyjae Spears, Kendre Miller, Keaton Mitchell, Devin Singletary

Roschon, Allgeier, Davis, Lloyd, Spears, Miller, and Mitchell are all RBs that I really like but are behind RB touch dominators. I would call them 'Yeah but' RBs. YEAH, Roschon is the best fit to be the goal line back in Chicago, BUT they have a lot of weapons, and the money the Bears paid Swift means he's getting most of the touches. YEAH, Allgeier is a very good back who could be a starter on many teams, BUT he's behind my #1 RB. Mitchell is a bit of an outlier from the rest of the group in that he can produce with few touches as a back built in the same mold as Achane as a breakaway speed, homerun-hitting type of back, but he's coming off an ACL tear. Davis and Lloyd will likely be 'change of pace' backs for Cook and Jacobs to start, but the talent offers way more. The young backs in this tier have talent, and the talent shines through in most cases, but the hill is more challenging to climb than the guys above them.

I also have Mostert and Singletary in this group because I think longevity is their 'Yeah, but'. Mostert is over 30, the Dolphins have drafted his replacement in Wright, and he's a free agent after this season, but he's coming off a season in which he was RB4 overall and was injury-free. Singletary is coming off a great season in Houston, but the downgrade of offenses is steep and caps his ceiling even if he is given more touches than he has had before, and his contract isn't impossible to get out of quickly.

Tier 6 - Upside shots and role players
Jaleel McLaughlin, Bucky Irving, Tyrone Tracy, Tank Bigsby, Kimani Vidal, J.K. Dobbins, Antonio Gibson, Khlalil Herbert, Gus Edwards, Braelon Allen, Chuba Hubbard, Miles Sanders, Rico Dowdle, Dameon Pierce, Zack Moss, Ezekiel Elliott, Alexander Mattison, Elijah Mitchell

There is a broader variety when we get down to this tier, but there are plenty of options depending on your needs. Hopefully, you'll be looking for 100% upside plays at your RB5. If that's the case, I would suggest the first five players on the list in McLaughlin, Irving, Tracy, Bigsby, Vidal, and then others like Allen, Dowdle, Pierce, and Mitchell. Vidal and Dowdle have a chance to be as high as one and as low as 3 for the majority of the season, but the rest I see as firm 'B' backs to an A. Rookies Irving, Tracy, and Allen should all be able to win the immediate backup job in camp and get run, but I don't expect any of them to earn more than 115 touches without an injury. McLaughlin is my favorite member of this group, but the additions of Estime and spending big money on UDFA Blake Watson have made me raise an eyebrow at his job security. I was ready to write Bigsby off after a disastrous rookie campaign, but the Jags didn't add outside of speedy special teamer Keilan Robinson, so he's getting another shot. I'm probably just being hard-headed, but I don't want to write off Dameon Pierce completely. Maybe he will take a jump, but if we don't see an improvement, he won't last long in the league. Mitchell might be the best RB in this tier, but he's behind CMC and won't see enough work to be dependable on a week-to-week basis.

If you are looking for contributors in this range, we also have them in Dobbins, Gibson, Herbert, Edwards, Hubbard, Sanders, Moss, Elliott, and Mattison. Dobbins and Edwards are following OC Greg Roman to LA and competing for the #1 job with each other. Dobbins has the broadest range of anyone here; as a former high draft pick whose injuries have plagued him, he could be getting his career back on track, or he can't beat out Edwards, and he's cut before the season starts. I think Edwards will have Vidal breathing down his neck as a backup or 3rd, either way. Gibson, Moss, and Mattison I see as backups to better options. Moss is the closest to having a shot to be a number 1, but I believe in Chase Brown to build that separation. Herbert is strange because he's the backup to the guy they are building the run game around in Swift, but Roschon is the likely goal line back; he's a UFA after this season and would benefit from a change of scenery, in my opinion. New coach Dave Canales could shake up the balance between Hubbard and Sanders for touches, but I think Brooks is the leader at the end of the season, so they are battling for a backup role. The Cowboys are returning to Zeke, but I'm not sure that will work out.

Tier 7 - Handcuffs and Dart Throws
Audric Estime, Will Shipley, Deuce Vaughn, Dylan Laube, Evan Hull, D'Ernest Johnson, Kenneth Gainwell, Ty Chandler, Isaiah Davis, Justice Hill, Israel Abanikanda, A.J. Dillon, Michael Carter, Kareem Hunt, D'Onta Foreman, Jamaal Williams

We're getting dicey. I think the young guys here, like Estime, Shipley, Vaughn, Laube, Hull, Davis, and Abainkanda, are the type of backs who can earn roles. For Shipley, Laube, and Abanikanda, it's a receiving-down role with room to grow. Estime, Hull, and Davis are suited for short-yardage and goal-line work, again with room to grow.

The rest of the guys here don't have youth on their side, but they seem to earn touches. Each of D'Ernest, Gainwell, Chandler, Hill, Dillon, Hunt, Foreman, and Williams had over 100 touches last season. Carter didn't get there, but I like him in an eventual third-down role that can flirt with RB3/4 range at his top end. Being ranked here means the bottom can fall out for any of these guys quickly.

WIDE RECEIVERS

WR isn't deep; it's an arms race. Drafting WRs early is the smart idea in Dynasty anyway because they have much longer career spans than RBs. This position gives us a little grace between the low end of WR2 and the high end of WR4. That's the section in the draft where I will wait and see what the board does. Any way it breaks, there's going to be somebody coming at a value if you choose to wait. There's a bit of a 'queasy dip' in the range after WR5, so I don't want to take more than WR6 shots after my top 65 WRs are gone. That said, I feel like the next 65 WRs are all in the same 'range of outcomes'. That's a little tongue-in-cheek, but the tiers have less separation from me, with young wide receivers with all kinds of upside and many guys who are vets who still have gas in the tank!

Tier 1 - #1 Overall Range
CeeDee Lamb, Justin Jefferson, Ja'Marr Chase, Amon-Ra St. Brown

The elite WRs are going into their prime! All four of these guys were WR1s in PPG last season. Jefferson only played ten games last year, but he finished averaging 24.3 PPG over the last three games, with Nick Mullens at QB. Lamb's four seasons in the NFL have seen him go from WR3 in his rookie season, WR2 in his second season, and in the last two seasons, he was 7th overall and 1st overall. Lamb can't get any higher than 1st at WR, but the Cowboys might rely on the passing game even more this season, given the issues at RB. Chase has finished as a WR1 in PPG in all 3 of his NFL seasons, and Amon-Ra started as a WR3 and has been a WR1 in the last two seasons with an offense that looks very strong! Young, proven, heavily targeted WRs with even more room to grow make them the first batch of players selected in Dynasty Drafts.

Tier 2 - Rookies with #1 Overall Upside
Marvin Harrison Jr., Malik Nabers

This rookie class has so many WRs, and Harrison and Nabers are the head of the class. The only reason they aren't in the top tier is because those guys all have a track record in the NFL. If your strategy is 'youth-based,' these guys can reach the top of your list. Harrison and Nabers become instant number-one WRs for their offenses, and I expect them to be in the WR1s neighborhood as rookies. Harrison is a touch safer because we've seen Kyler Murray feed some monster WRs. Daniel Jones is returning from a knee injury; his most prolific WR has been Darius Slayton. I think Nabers is potentially good enough to be QB-proof, so I'm not disappointed if I have to 'settle' for Nabers.

Tier 3 - The Reason picking low in the 1st is fine
A.J. Brown, Tyreek Hill, Garrett Wilson, Chris Olave, Rome Odunze, Puka Nacua

Brown has been a WR1 in 3 of his five seasons, and he's only 27. The only reason he's not in the Top Tier is because he's two years older than all of those guys. Tyreek Hill has been in Miami for two seasons and finished 2nd and 3rd among WRs in those two seasons. The only reason he's down here is he's 30 and talked about retiring early many times. It seems Tyreek can play longer if he wants, and he's been collecting kids like Pokemon recently.

Wilson, Olave, Odunze, and Nacua are all young and talented. Wilson has produced two WR3 seasons, but he obviously hasn't had a competent QB to rely on, and (hopefully) he will get a season with Aaron Rodgers under center, and we should see, at the very least, a bit more production. Olave gets the same quarterback in New Orleans, but last season's back half had him right on the borderline of the WR1/WR2 area, and I think he can step into it this season. Odunze is another impressive rookie who has drawn comparisons to Larry Fitzgerald coming out of Washington. Odunze is a stud; he will be the number-one wide receiver in Chicago for a long time. I'm a big fan of D.J. Moore, but Odunze has the potential to dominate for a long time. Nacua lit the NFL on fire in his rookie season, finishing 4th overall among WRs and 6th in PPG. The only tiny concern about Nacua is that he went from a WR1 to a WR2 average when Kupp was healthy, but the floor is still high.

Tier 4 - I want my 2nd WR from this group
DJ Moore, Jaylen Waddle, Nico Collins, Brandon Aiyuk, Michael Pittman, DK Metcalf, Tee Higgins, Drake London, DeVonta Smith, Jordan Addison

There are a few #1 WRs in their offense from this tier in Collins, Aiyuk, Pittman, Metcalf, and London. Collins was an absolute stud last season, finishing 7th in PPG. The only slight knock I have for Collins is that he averaged four more points per game without Dell, who will be back, and they added Diggs. Aiyuk is still a stud, but who knows how long he will last in SF with all the trade rumors. Aiyuk moving could be beneficial, but it might hurt a lot, so it clouds him moving forward. I love Pittman; he was super underrated going into last season and produced career-highs in receptions and yards. The Colts did add Adonai Mitchell in the draft and get Jonathan Taylor healthy to start the year, but if Richardson clicks, they could all be undervalued right now. Metcalf and London will be going into new offensive systems, but they both had over 100 targets last year and might be in line for more this season.

The #2's in this tier are mixed with #1's because they should all be viewed as high-volume targets. Moore and Waddle are my highest guys in this tier, and I think Odunze will move past Moore quickly while Waddle is behind Hill until he retires. However, the guy next to them makes these guys better. Higgins (Chase), Smith (Brown), and Addison (Jefferson) all could be the #1 for so many teams, at least ten teams by my count right now. Maybe I'm too high on Higgins, but I like him. he's only older than 3 of the ten guys in this tier and has four years of experience.

Tier 5 - The Deep Tier
Xavier Worthy, Keon Coleman, Ladd McConkey, Brian Thomas, Cooper Kupp, Davante Adams, Mike Evans, Stefon Diggs, Deebo Samuel, Zay Flowers. Jayden Reed, Jaxon Smith-Njigba. George Pickens, Rashee Rice. Tank Dell. Christain Watson

This is my aforementioned 'wait and take who falls' section of the draft. To be clear, I already want to have 2 WRs before getting here, but I'm not reaching if I don't. We'll start with the rookies in Worthy, Coleman, McConkey and Thomas. The great thing about this group is that they are all connected to stud QBs and could quickly become the #1 WR! Worthy has the most extensive range of outcomes due to his stature, but he reminds me of Tyreek so much that I'm all aboard the hype train! Coleman and McConkey aren't facing an uphill battle to lead their team in targets. Brian Thomas landed in Jacksonville, and I think he's already better than Kirk, but they also have Engram. It might be a little harder for him to earn it than the others, but I had him ranked highest of all these guys going in so I believe in him.

The old men of this section can still be high-end WR2s for the next two years, but their decline will obviously start sooner than the other guys in this tier. Kupp missed five games last season, so he might be off some drafters' lists. Kupp did average over 18 PPG in his last five, which would have been WR7 overall on the season. Evans is coming off a WR1 season with his QB returning; Deebo was right behind him as WR13 overall, and even though there were a lot of rumors, he's still in San Francisco. Davante is the oldest man by six months, but the Raiders have a better quarterback in Minshew (surprising to say), and with Jacobs gone, they are likely to throw a bit more this season. If no one steps up and really earns the lead-back role for Vegas, we could see even more passing.

The end of this tier has Flowers, Reed, JSN, Pickens, Rice, Dell, and Watson. Each of these WRs is under 25, and I'm lower than the consensus ECR on all but Watson. I still really like all of them, but I have minor concerns. For instance, Flowers didn't have Mark Andrews to compete for targets in 7 games, and here comes Derrick Henry to have them run even more. Reed played better without Watson (14.4-11.3), and the difference made him go from a WR2 to a WR4. Pickens and JSN are moving toward more run-heavy offenses (Pickens, for sure, JSN, I could be mistaken). Rice is pissing away his NFL career quickly with off-the-field nonsense, and if he doesn't get on track quickly, it could be over soon. Buy him low rice if you're confident he'll turn it around; I just don't. Dell set the league on first to start, but his size concerns showed up, and he missed the last six games of the season. I really like Watson, but he's played 23 of 34 games in his two-year career. There is still plenty of 'meat on the bone' here for this young group to reach their fullest potential.

Tier 6 - Oldies but Goodies
Terry McLaurin, Amari Cooper, Chris Godwin, Keenan Allen, Christian Kirk, Diontate Johnson, Calvin Ridley

Now, I will make some groups, but they are clear breaks for me. I'm buying if I can get one of these WRs, all 27+, as my WR4 or 5. McLaurin is the only guy that doesn't have at least a handful of missed games. Allen is older than the rest but was WR3 overall in PPG last season. I like SO many of the rookies still to come, but these guys should all have 120 targets this year, and, outside of *maybe* Allen, they should all have more than 1 season left.

Tier 7 - Production vs Potential
Adonai Mitchell, Ja'Lynn Polk, Xavier Legeette, Jakobi Meyers, Courtland Sutton, Jermaine Burton, Ricky Pearsall, Troy Franklin, Javon Baker

I'm likelier to take a shot on one of the rookies here. I think Mitchell will be on the field quickly and a lot to start, so he's my favorite here. Polk, Legette, Franklin, and Baker all go into offenses that are looking for a true #1, so the opportunity will be there very quickly. Burton and Pearsall might have to wait to contribute, but I believe in both. Meyers and Sutton are both in the age range of the previous tier, but I'm worried about them for this season. Sutton wants to be traded, and any spot he goes will likely be a downgrade for targets. Meyers, I like, but Bowers will become the #2 for targets quickly for the Raiders.

Tier 8 - Lower ceiling, higher floor
Jameson Williams, Jerry Jeudy. Josh Downs, DeAndre Hopkins, Josh Palmer, Jahan Dotson, Quentin Johnston, Marquise Brown, Dontayvion Wicks, Romeo Doubs, Rashid Shaheed

There's a big mix here, so we'll start with the biggest upside play: Jameson Williams. I think Jameson is higher than this ranking, but the hill is steeper to climb, with weapons like LaPorta and Gibbs being so dominant. Even if Williams gets everything on track, there will be a lot of mouths to feed. Jeudy is tricky; I really hate that he couldn't make it work in Denver. Even if Jeudy is much better than Denver made him look he's still behind Cooper, Moore, and probably Njoku on a run-1st offense. Downs, Palmer, Dotson, and Johnston are all talented enough to move well beyond this tier, but the clock will click really fast if they don't make a jump this season. Hopkins has nothing left to prove; he's on a void contract after making $12 mil this season, maybe he will go ring chasing, but this year is all that's guaranteed. Marquise Brown, Dontayvion Wicks, Rome Doubs, and Rashid Shaheed are all probably 2nd at best (and more likely 3rd) in target share, which will waiver from game to game, but they are still VERY talented. Doubs and Wicks will compete for targets in GB, but they are both younger than Brown and Shaheed by a year and a half.

Tier 9 - Crypto and Thrift
Khalil Shakir, Gabriel Davis, Jalen McMillan, Luke McCaffrey, Roman Wilson, Mike Williams, Demario Douglas, Malachi Corley, Michael Wilson, Jalin Hyatt, Marvin Mims, Elijah Moore, Adam Thielen, Tyler Lockett

Now, I'm really more inclined to take a risk, but any of these guys can be a #2 option as soon as this year. Shakir, Davis, McMillian, McCaffrey, Wilson, Douglas, Corley, and Wilson are likely to be 3rd or 4th in targets behind 2 WRs and an RB or TE but are talented enough for more. Williams, Moore (concussions), Thielen, and Lockett are going to be WR2s in their offenses this year, but nothing beyond this season is a lock for them. Hyatt and Mims are big-play types of WRs who can earn a good role but are likely to be hit-or-miss for their career.

Tier 10 - Best of the Rest
Rashod Bateman, Andrei Iosivas, Zay Jones, Tyler Boyd, Curtis Samuel, Noah Brown, Brandin Cooks, Devontez Walker, Malik Washington, Kendrick Bourne, Darius Slayton, Treylon Burks, Michael Thomas, A.T. Perry, Tre Tucker, Darnell Mooney, Josh Reynolds, Wan'Dale Robinson, Odell Beckham, Jonathan Mingo, Charlie Jones, Parker Washington, Bo Melton

Starting with the upside, there is still time for guys like Rashod Bateman, Treylon Burks, Darnell Mooney, and Jonathan Mingo to win a big-time role, but ranking them here means I probably wouldn't take the bet. Iosivas, Walker, M Washington, Tucker, Jones, P Washington, and Melton are all talented WRs buried on the depth chart. Z Jones, Boyd, Samuel, Bourne, Thomas, Reynolds, and Beckham are old men who can still contribute if you're looking for less risk here. Slayton and Perry are probably WR3s (not target) in their offense this season, and I think that's where they belong.

TIGHT ENDS

TE is deep! There are definitely tiers, and things can look a little shallower in two TE leagues or TE premium, but there's a lot to like here. LaPorta is the only TE going in the first two rounds of 12-man drafts early in draft season. Only four are going in the first four rounds, but 7 TEs go between rounds 5 and 8, so if there is a specific one you want from that 2nd tier. Even if you decide to wait longer than that, there are plenty of deeper options. The main issue with TE is not talent; many teams have talented TEs. It's about them actually seeing the field and earning targets. Last season, 60 WRs averaged at least five targets per game, and only 17 TEs did. The number drops even lower when we talk snap% to only 13 TEs getting snaps at a 70% clip or higher. Cade Otton was the only TE over 84% and the only one with over 1000 snaps. I feel confident enough about the depth of the other positions to take an early TE, but the following two tiers are very forgiving if we are to miss out on our top choices.

Tier 1 - Long Term Top Targets
Sam LaPorta, Trey McBride, Brock Bowers, Mark Andrews

LaPorta is the consensus #1 Overall TE after his unbelievable rookie season! Only Kelce (33) and Hockenson (January ACL/MCL surgery) averaged more points than LaPorta, and no one totaled more than him. Current ECR has LaPorta at 15, and I'm lower than that at 24, but he's a second-round pick either way in 12-man formats.

McBride really took off in his sophomore season. Kyler Murray returned from his injury in Week 10, and after that, McBride was the third most-targeted TE and 14th most-targeted player. Marvin Harrison Jr. will take a lot of targets, but McBride should be able to work well off that, and I would assume he's in for more than 3 TDs.

Buy the hype on Bowers. Bowers is INCREDIBLE with the ball in his hands, so much so that Kirby Smart said he would have been the best RB on Georgia if they played him in that position. Raiders OC Luke Getsy has already spoken on how Bowers opens up the offense. He can easily be the #1 TE as early as this season and has an incredibly bright future.

Mark Andrews played in only ten games, battling through injuries, and was still 5th in PPG. Andrews is the oldest by a lot here, but he's been a top-5 scoring TE for every season since 2019. I think Andrews has at least a few seasons left. He's still the #1 receiving option for Baltimore, and I'm excited to see how he works with Derrick Henry.

Tier 2 - High Volume Targets
Dalton Kincaid, T.J. Hockenson, Kyle Pitts, Travis Kelce, David Njoku, George Kittle, Evan Engram

Kincaid and Pitts represent the youthful upside of this tier and I might be low on them. Kincaid is seeing a surge in rankings because there's more opportunity this year with Diggs and Davis leaving 241 Targets behind in Buffalo. I'm 'lower' on Kincaid because his best stretch was when Knox went down but I'm still a big believer in him and the opportunity is there for him to take a big step this year. Pitts had an unbelievable Rookie season but hasn't been able to match it in the next two seasons. I'm holding out hope that new OC Zac Robinson is going to utilize Pitts properly and bring his value back up to where it should be. This may read as me being low on these guys but I still have them at 5 and 7 among TEs.

T.J. Hockenson is an absolute stud, but he's coming off a major injury (ACL+MCL tear) in late January. Hock is going to miss a big chunk of this season, and this is a big injury. I assume he's going to come back and look similar, but it's never a guarantee. If there were no injury, Hockenson would be #2 right behind LaPorta.

Kelce, Kittle, and Engram are all studs who will be 30+ going into this season, and with TE being one of the most brutal positions on the field, nothing is guaranteed beyond this season. Kelce is still amazing but took a step back towards the rest of the top group last season (14.7 PPR PPG, lowest average since 2016) instead of living at the top by himself. Kittle is still one of the best TEs around and was the only TE with over 1000 yards last season but he feels like he's been banged up and playing through injuries for a while now. Kittle has lost a little bit every year since peaking in 2018, and the cliff is getting closer and closer. Engram led all TEs last season in targets and had a career-high in receiving yards. I think being 31 caps Engram's longevity, but he still has a ton of production left.

Tier 3 - Clear #1 TEs but fighting for Targets
Cole Kmet, Jake Ferguson, Dallas Goedert, Dalton Schultz, Luke Musgrave, Ben Sinnott, Ja'Tavion Sanders, Isaiah Likely, Tucker Kraft, Pat Freiermuth

The break between Tiers 3 and 4 is fairly small to me. The difference is that these guys have TE1 upside, and the next tier probably doesn't. Kmet, Goedert, Schultz, Musgrave, Likely, Kraft, and Friermuth are all capable of more, but they will firmly be between the third and fourth targets on their team. Musgrave and Kraft are contending with each other and Isaiah Likely is behind Mark Andrews.

Ferguson, Sinnott, and Sanders all have a shot at seeing #2 target shares as early as this season. The Cowboys didn't add a significant pass catcher, and the Panthers did trade for Johnson and draft Leggette, but with a new coaching staff, the pecking order is wide open. Sinnott has Ertz in front of him, but Ertz is old, and Sinnott was a second-round pick. A quick change for Washington wouldn't be surprising at all.

Tier 4 - Talented but unreliable
Michael Mayer, Chig Okonkwo, Taysom Hill, Hunter Henry, Cade Otton, Juwan Johnson, Greg Dulcich, Jelani Woods, Dawson Knox

Mayer, Woods, and Knox are talented enough to be in the higher tiers, but they are pretty buried in the pecking order as the second TE on their team. I don't think Mayer is going to drop as much as his ADP suggests, but he's definitely lost value with Bowers coming in. Knox had it last year when the Bills drafted Kincaid, and Woods has to earn it again coming off a knee injury.

Chig Okonkwo and Greg Dulcich are both going into the season as #1 TE options but they have obstacles to overcome for targets. For Okonkwo it's fighting Hopkins, Ridley, Boyd and Pollard for targets, and for Dulcich, it's getting healthy and moving past Trautman on the depth chart.

Hill is turning 34 before the season starts. He's losing steam on the rushing side, and Juwan Johnson is still ahead of him for targets. Hunter Henry has had to battle through injuries the last few seasons and ended 2023 on the IR. Henry will still be able to get targets with New England, but the clock is ticking. Cade Otton led the league in Snaps and Snap% but only put up a TE3 season in PPG, so he needs to stay down here.

Tier 5 - Everyone else
Tyler Conklin, Noah Fant, Noah Gray, Erick All, Luke Schoonmaker, Brenton Strange, Daniel Bellinger, Theo Johnson, Cade Stover, Jonnu Smith, Darren Waller, Tyler Higbee

Tyler Conklin is a good TE who should probably be higher than this, but I like all 3 of the guys behind him on the Jets depth chart as well. Fant, Bellinger, and Jonnu Smith are starting TEs who aren't going to earn a large chunk of targets, but they'll all start. Gray, All, Schoonmaker, Strange, Johnson, and Stover are all great, young receiving options buried on their team depth chart. Waller and Higbee have had good careers, but they're getting old for the position. Waller might retire before the season. Higbee isn't much younger than Waller, he had major knee surgery in February and probably won't be ready to start the season.

Chapter 12

NFL Team Previews 2024

AFC East

Buffalo Bills

Key additions: Notable additions to the Buffalo Bills roster include WR Curtis Samuel, S Taylor Rapp, S Mike Edwards, OT La'el Collins, WR Mack Hollins, and QB Mitch Trubisky. These new players are expected to bring a fresh dynamic to the team's offense and defense, potentially influencing their performance in the upcoming season.

Key losses: However, the Buffalo Bills have also faced significant setbacks in the offseason. The team has bid farewell to key players such as WR Stefon Diggs, WR Gabe Davis, CB Tre'Davious White, S Jordan Poyer, S Micah Hyde, and EDGE Leonard Floyd. These departures could potentially disrupt the team's structure and performance, raising concerns about their upcoming season.

Key draft picks: WR Keon Coleman, S Cole Bishop, DT DeWayne Carter, RB Ray Davis

With the significant changes that Buffalo has undergone in the offseason, it's a compelling question to consider if they will have enough firepower to return to the playoffs in 2024. Salary cap issues prevented the team from re-signing several key veterans, including wideout Gabe Davis and most of their existing secondary unit in Jordan Poyer, Micah Hyde, and Tre'Davious White. To complicate matters, Buffalo traded All-Pro Stefon Diggs to the Houston Texans in exchange for multiple draft picks. The team is banking on the additions of Curtis Samuel and rookie Keon Coleman from Florida State to fill their gaps, but it remains to be seen if that will be enough. Pay attention to Buffalo's increased reliance on James Cook in the ground game and their strategic use of tight ends Dalton Kincaid and Dawson Knox. The balanced script that offensive coordinator Joe Brady used in 2023 will continue, but there's a real possibility that Buffalo may not finish first in the AFC East for the first time in five years.

Miami Dolphins

Key additions: EDGE Shaquil Barret, LB Jordyn Brooks, CB Kendall Fuller, S Jordan Poyer, TE Jonnu Smith

Key losses: DL Christian Wilkins, CB Xavien Howard, EDGE Andrew Van Ginkel, LB Jerome Baker, S Brandon Jones, EDGE Melvin Engram, EDGE Emmanuel Ogbah

Key draft picks: EDGE Chop Robinson, RB Jaylen Wright, EDGE Mohamed Kamara, WR Malik Washington

Despite an early postseason departure in the Wild Card round against the Kansas City Chiefs, the Dolphins had a very successful 11-6 season. Miami led the NFL in total offensive touchdowns (61) thanks to the quick-strike ability of their speedy weaponry and creative play calling. Arguably the most dynamic offense in the NFL, Miami boasted multiple 1,000-yard receiving threats (Tyreek Hill and Jaylen Waddle) and a 1,000-yard rusher in Raheem Mostert (with breakout rookie De'Von Achane not far behind). For the team to take the next step forward, their completely reformed defense must gel quickly as they wait for star pass rusher Jaelan Phillips to recover from an Achilles injury. If Miami's defense struggles again, Fantasy managers can expect plenty of shootouts and high point totals—a promising prospect. Tua Tagovailoa led the league in passing yards in 2023 (4,624) and has solidified himself as a backend QB1 for Fantasy purposes.

New England

Key additions: QB Jacoby Brissett, RB Antonio Gibson, LB Sione Takitaki, WR K.J. Osborn, TE Austin Hooper

Key losses: QB Mac Jones, RB Ezekiel Elliott, WR Devante Parker, TE Mike Gesicki, LB Mack Wilson, CB Jalen Mills, CB J.C. Jackson, ST Matthew Slater

Key draft picks: QB Drake Maye, WR Ja'Lynn Polk, WR Javon Baker, QB Joe Milton III

Changes abound in Foxboro. For the first time in 24 years, the Patriots will have a new head coach on the sidelines in Jerod Mayo, and the team also enters 2024 with a brand new quarterback room of Jacoby Brissett and third-overall pick Drake Maye. The team would greatly benefit by allowing Maye to redshirt this season, focusing on improving his accuracy issues and footwork. Whether Brissett will keep the team afloat until that happens is another question. New England had the weakest offense in the entire league last year, finishing in the bottom seven in both passing and rushing totals while scoring the third-fewest touchdowns. The Patriots are banking on significant production from rookie receivers Ja'Lynn Polk and Javon Baker, coupled with the healthy return of running back Rhamondre Stevenson to keep the team competitive. We aren't holding our breath.

New York

Key additions: WR Mike Williams, EDGE Haason Reddick, OT Tyron Smith, OT Morgan Moses, QB Tyrod Taylor, CB Isaian Oliver, DL Javon Kinlaw, DL Leki Fotu

Key losses: EDGE Bryce Huff, S Jordan Whitehead, DL Quinton Jefferson, WR Randall Cobb, CB Bryce Hall, OT Mekhi Becton

Key draft picks: OT Olu Fashanu, WR Malachi Corley, RB Braelon Allen, QB Jordan Travis, RB Isaiah Davis, CB Qwan'tex Stiggers

If you ever want to hear the sound of hope physically leaving someone's body, listen to a Jets fan's reaction to Aaron Rodgers tearing his Achilles in week one. After just four snaps, New York's entire season was derailed and continued to sputter under the quarterback carousel of Zach Wilson, Trevor Siemian, and Tim Boyle. Thankfully, the team has concentrated on moving forward rather than lamenting the past. Determined to improve their offense, the Jets made it a point to bring in additional playmakers for Rodgers, signing Mike Williams and drafting Western Kentucky standout Malachi Corley. Additionally, they bolstered their offensive line with Morgan Moses and first-round pick Olu Fashanu to keep Rodgers upright and not permanently looking over his shoulder. Running back Breece Hall eclipsed 1,500 total yards from scrimmage last year despite being "eased" back into action, and wide receiver Garrett Wilson miraculously broke the 1,000-yard mark despite the situation under center. Both players are a real threat to finish atop their positions in Fantasy this year.

AFC North

Baltimore

Key additions: RB Derrick Henry, QB Josh Johnson, OT Josh Jones

Key losses: LB Patrick Queen, RB Gus Edwards, OT Morgan Moses, S Geno Stone, EDGE Jadeveon Clowney, OG Kevin Zeitler, QB Tyler Huntley, WR Devin Duvernay, RB Dalvin Cook, RB J.K. Dobbins

Key draft picks: CB Nate Wiggins, LB Adisa Isaac, OT Roger Rosengarten, WR Devontez Walker, RB Rasheen Ali

The stars were aligned for Baltimore to return to the Super Bowl for the first time since 2012 after finishing as the top seed in the AFC. However, several undisciplined mistakes allowed Kansas City to pull off the upset instead, dropping Lamar Jackson's postseason record to 2-4. The Ravens will return as favorites to make the postseason but must adjust to changes made within the backfield and offensive line. Following the departure of Gus Edwards, Dalvin Cook, and J.K. Dobbins, Baltimore made one of the biggest splashes in free agency by signing eight-year veteran Derrick Henry. Henry has shown little signs of slowing down despite his overwhelming usage and led the NFL in rushing attempts (280) last year, finishing second in rushing yards (1,167). The losses of guards Kevin Zeitler and John Simpson, along with tackle Morgan Moses, will test the capabilities of Henry and Jackson on a team determined to run the ball early and often. Two-time league MVP Jackson must carry his strong regular season play into January and beyond to shake the narrative that he struggles when it matters most.

Cincinnati

Key additions: RB Zack Moss, TE Mike Gesicki, OT Trent Brown, DT Sheldon Rankins, S Vonn Bell, S Geno Stone

Key losses: RB Joe Mixon, DT D.J. Reader, WR Tyler Boyd, TE Irv Smith, CB Chidobe Awuzie, OT Jonah Williams, S Nick Scott

Key draft picks: OT Amarius Mims, DT Kris Jenkins, WR Jermaine Burton, DT McKinnley Jackson, TE Erick All, CB Josh Newton, TE Tanner McLachlan

Joe Burrow labored through the first month of 2023 with a lingering calf strain and then suffered a season-ending wrist injury during Week 11 against Baltimore. His absence doomed the team's playoff hopes despite the admirable play of backup Jake Browning. To give Burrow additional protection, Cincinnati signed veteran Trent Brown and drafted his heir apparent, Georgia tackle Amarius Mims, in the first round. The Bengals also moved on from running back Joe Mixon and signed Zack Moss as an early-down replacement to pair with Chase Brown. Moss shined during his tenure with Indianapolis last year, averaging over 21 touches and close to 100 total yards per game. The explosive tandem of All-Pro options Jamar Chase and Tee Higgins remain in place, rounding out a lethal offense that rivals any in the league. If Burrow stays upright the entire year, the Bengals can contend for the AFC North title and represent the conference in the Super Bowl.

Cleveland

Key additions: WR Jerry Jeudy, DL Quinton Jefferson, QB Jameis Winston, QB Tyler Huntley, RB Nyheim Hines, LB Devin Bush, LB Jordan Hicks, RB D'Onta Foreman

Key losses: QB Joe Flacco, RB Kareem Hunt, LB Sione Takitaki, LB Anthony Walker, DL Jordan Elliott, WR Marquise Goodwin, TE Harrison Bryant

Key draft picks: DT Michael Hall Jr., OG Zak Zinter, WR Jamari Thrash

Early returns of the massive Deshaun Watson trade have not been particularly encouraging for Cleveland, to put things mildly. Formerly a top-five option for Fantasy purposes, Watson has failed to recapture the same magic he had during his first three seasons with Houston, and one has to wonder if he will ever return to form. In the first six games of 2023, before he landed on the season-ending IR with a shoulder injury, Watson averaged just 185 yards per game and a paltry 6.5 yards per attempt. Even more frustratingly, any semblance of his rushing upside has evaporated. Thankfully, the team still has plenty of offensive talent surrounding Watson to kick-start him this year, including Amari Cooper, Elijah Moore, David Njoku, and newly acquired wideout Jerry Jeudy. Cleveland's running game took a significant step back after Nick Chubb's gruesome knee injury, but the Browns hope he will return early in 2024 to provide stability behind Watson. This team will only go as far as Watson allows them to.

Pittsburgh

Key additions: QB Justin Fields, QB Russell Wilson, LB Patrick Queen, CB Donte Jackson, S DeShon Elliott, DL Dean Lowry, WR Cordarrell Patterson, WR Van Jefferson

Key losses: QB Kenny Pickett, Mason Rudolph, QB Mitch Trubisky, WR Diontae Johnson, WR Allen Robinson, LB Mykal Walker, CB Patrick Peterson

Key draft picks: OG Troy Fautanu, C Zach Frazier, WR Roman Wilson, LB Payton Wilson, OG Mason McCormick

If asked what has changed about the Pittsburgh Steelers from last year, the simple answer is everything. The team moved on from perpetual disappointment Kenny Pickett in favor of an "island of misfit toys" approach between Russell Wilson and Justin Fields. Wilson is the presumptive starter of the two players, but keep a close eye on the training camp battle. The Steelers also gutted the receiving core, replacing Diontae Johnson and Allen Robinson in favor of veterans Van Jefferson and Cordarrelle Patterson and rookie Michigan standout Roman Wilson. A devastating weapon out of the slot and a perfect complement to George Pickens on the outside, Wilson has drawn comparisons to Tyler Lockett, a former Wilson teammate. Fantasy managers are hoping that new offensive coordinator Arthur Smith will be more aggressive in pushing the ball downfield than he was during his tenure in Atlanta. Fingers crossed.

AFC South

Houston

Key additions: WR Stefon Diggs, RB Joe Mixon, EDGE Danielle Hunter, DL Denico Autry, DL Mario Edwards, LB Azeez Al-Shaair, CB Jeff Okudah, CB C.J. Henderson

Key losses: RB Devin Singletary, EDGE Jonathan Greenard, DT Sheldon Rankins, DT Maliek Collins, OT George Fant, LB Denzel Perryman, LB Blake Cashman, CB Steven Nelson, EDGE Jerry Hughes

Key draft picks: CB Kamari Lassiter, OT Blake Fisher, S Calen Bullock, TE Cade Stover, LB Jamal Hill, RB Jawhar Jordan

All aboard the hype train. Last season's media darlings, Houston had a surprise turnaround year because of their tremendous draft class, boasting *both* the Offensive (C.J. Stroud) and Defensive (Will Anderson) Rookies of the Year. Stroud finished within the top 8 at the position in passing yards (4,108) and passer rating (100.8) and led Houston to a blowout playoff win over Cleveland. The Texans were incredibly active in free agency, signing veteran Joe Mixon as a replacement for Devin Singletary and then shoring up their defense line with the additions of Danielle Hunter, Denico Autry, and Mario Edwards. Additionally, Houston traded for disgruntled wideout Stefon Diggs from Buffalo, providing Stroud with another weapon to wreak havoc on intermediate routes. Diggs's presence lowers the fantasy ceilings of Collins and Dell, placing all three in low-end WR2 territory. It will be interesting to see if Houston can replicate their success or take another step forward. This is a very well-rounded team.

Indianapolis

Key additions: Joe Flacco, DL Raekwon Davis, RB Trey Sermon

Key losses: QB Gardner Minshew, RB Zack Moss, WR Isaiah McKenzie

Key draft picks: EDGE Laiatu Latu, WR Adonai Mitchell, OT Matt Goncalves, WR Anthony Gould

The Colts selected Anthony Richardson fourth overall in the 2023 draft, hoping that the 6'4, 244 lb. athletic marvel would be the second coming of Cam Newton. What they received was far from it. Richardson was forced to miss time in each of the four games he started before being placed on IR with a season-ending AC joint sprain. A focus was made during the offseason, teaching Richardson to better protect himself from the speed and violence at the NFL level. Hopefully, those lessons will sink in quickly. If healthy, Richardson's upside rivals any quarterback in the league. A fully healthy Richardson and running back Jonathan Taylor will create a rushing attack that will cause severe headaches for defensive coordinators if they can stay on the field. After consecutive seasons of underperforming, Taylor will look to return to his 2021 statistics, where he finished with over 2,100 scrimmage yards and 20 total touchdowns. Michael Pittman Jr., Josh Downs, and Texas rookie Adonai Mitchell present a formidable trio of weapons at all levels down the field. Prepare for a bounce-back year from the Colts.

Jacksonville

Key additions: DL Arik Armstead, WR Gabe Davis, S Darnell Savage, G Ezra Cleveland, WR Devin Duvernay, C Mitch Morse, QB Mac Jones

Key losses: WR Calvin Ridley, S Rayshawn Jenkins, CB Darious Williams, EDGE K'Lavon Chaisson, WR Jamal Agnew

Key draft picks: WR Brian Thomas Jr., DT Maason Smith, CB Jarrian Jones, DT Jordan Jefferson, OT Javon Foster

"A riddle wrapped in a mystery inside an enigma" is an apt description of the Jaguars 2023 season. Jacksonville managed to have another late-season collapse and failed to clinch the AFC South, mainly in part due to the struggles of third-year quarterback Trevor Lawrence. Fantasy managers were hoping to see Lawrence take a significant step forward in the absence of disgraced coach Urban Meyer, but several mental mistakes, dropped passes, and costly turnovers led to him finishing as the QB13 on the year. The Jaguars receiver room has been retooled after the team signed Gabe Davis and Devin Duvernay in free agency, then added LSU product Brian Thomas Jr. in the first round. A large-bodied speedster that can make splash plays all over the field, all expectations are that Thomas will quickly ascend Jacksonville's depth chart to become the WR2 opposite Christian Kick. Their upgraded receiver core will complement a ground game led by Travis Etienne Jr., who was exceedingly boom-or-bust last year. A low-end RB1 for Fantasy, Etienne will look to secure his third consecutive 1,400 total-yard season.

Tennessee

Key additions: CB L'Jarius Sneed, RB Tony Pollard, WR Calvin Ridley, C Lloyd Cushenberry, DT Sebastian Joseph-Day, CB Chidobe Awuzie, LB Kenneth Murray, QB Mason Rudolph

Key losses: Derrick Henry, DL Denico Autry, QB Ryan Tannehill, LB Azeez Al-Shaair, CB Kristian Fulton, CB Sean Murphy-Bunting, S Terrell Edmunds, CB K'Von Wallace

Key draft picks: OT J.C. Latham, DT T'Vondre Sweat, LB Cedric Gray

After the Mike Vrabel era ended with a thud, Tennessee hired former Cincinnati Bengals offensive coordinator Brian Callahan as his replacement. Known for his prodigious offensive mind, Callahan will hope that his new WR-trio of Calvin Ridley, DeAndre Hopkins, and Treylon Burks can rival that of his former job. Will Levis enters his second season in the league as the Titan's unquestioned starter, and the additions of center Lloyd Cushenberry and first-round Alabama tackle J.C. Latham will afford him actual time in the pocket to allow plays to develop. He will operate under center with the committee of Tony Pollard and Tyjae Spears behind him after Derrick Henry left in free agency. Perhaps the biggest disappointment of the 2023 Fantasy season, Pollard will look to right the ship after finishing as the RB23, despite being drafted in the first round.

AFC West

Denver

Key additions: WR Josh Reynolds, DI Malcolm Roach, S Brandon Jones, LB Cody Barton, OT Matt Peart

Key losses: QB Russell Wilson, WR Jerry Jeudy, LB Josey Jewell, S Justin Simmons, C Lloyd Cushenberry, DL Jonathan Harris, DL Mike Purcell

Key draft picks: QB Bo Nix, EDGE Jonah Elliss, WR Troy Franklin, CB Kris Abrams-Draine, RB Audric Estime

Sometimes, one must rip off the band-aid and move on. Finally admitting that the Russell Wilson experiment was an unmitigated disaster, the Broncos released him in early March, eating a massive $85M in dead money over the next two seasons. Denver selected Bo Nix as his immediate replacement with the 12th overall pick in the draft. Nix is an ideal fit for head coach Sean Payton's offense, and he has the added benefit of throwing to his favorite target from Oregon, Troy Franklin. In a talented but crowded receiver room, Franklin will compete with Marvin Mims and Josh Reynolds for snaps opposite Courtland Sutton. Denver finished 2023 with the sixth-fewest passing attempts, fifth-fewest first-downs gained via the pass, and a paltry 7 YPA average. The team will need to try harder to push the ball downfield. Javonte Williams holds a tenuous grip over the starting role in the backfield and must return to his dynamic 2021 form to fend off Jaleel McLaughlin and rookie Audric Estime for snaps.

Kansas City

Key additions: WR Marquise Brown, TE Irv Smith, QB Carson Wentz

Key losses: L'Jarius Sneed, S Mike Edwards, C Nick Allegretti, LB Willie Gay, WR Marquez Valdes-Scantling, WR Mecole Hardman

Key draft picks: WR Xavier Worthy, OT Kingsley Suamataia, TE Jared Wiley, S Jaden Hicks

Even though the offense wasn't as dynamic as in prior years, the Chiefs silenced all doubters by repeating as Super Bowl champions last season. For Fantasy purposes, Patrick Mahomes fell short of his lofty career averages, finishing with just over 260 passing yards per game, the lowest mark in his career. A lack of a genuine deep threat also torpedoed his yards per attempt down to 6.9, and he became increasingly reliant upon Travis Kelce to move the offense up and down the field. Kansas City addressed this obvious shortcoming by signing Marquise Brown in free agency and drafting the fastest rookie receiver ever to enter the league, Xavier Worthy, from the University of Texas. Drawing comparisons to DeSean Jackson, he will see immediate, meaningful snaps with the Chiefs top receiver Rashee Rice facing a lengthy suspension. Behind Mahomes, Isaiah Pacheco finished as the RB14 in 2023, averaging over 20 touches and 100 total yards each game. He can go nuclear if defenses cannot load the box against him each week. The Chiefs are primed for another deep run into the playoffs.

Las Vegas

Key additions: QB Gardner Minshew, DL Christian Wilkins, RB Alexander Mattison

Key losses: RB Josh Jacobs, QB Jimmy Garoppolo, OT Jermaine Eluemunor, DT Jerry Tiller, DL Bilal Nichols, WR Hunter Renfrow, WR DeAndre Carter

Key draft picks: TE Brock Bowers, C Jackson Powers-Johnson, OT Delmar Glaze, CB Decamerion Richardson, LB Tommy Eichenberg, RB Dylan Laube

The Raiders finally came to their senses mid-season in 2023, firing inept head coach Josh McDaniels and replacing him with Antonio Pierce. The team responded by playing their hearts out and demanding that he be installed as the permanent option. All eyes in the preseason will be on the quarterback battle between Aidan O'Connell and journeyman Gardner Minshew. Whoever emerges victorious will throw from two tight end sets often, after the Raiders drafted Georgia standout Brock Bowers 13th overall. Bowers will run as a "slot" type tight end, with Michael Mayer being an in-line option, drawing coverage away from All-Pro receiver Davante Adams. Adams finished with the second-most targets in the NFL (175) last year and overcame poor quarterback play to post a 103-1,1144-8 split. He remains a high-end WR2. Running back Zamir White propelled fantasy managers into the playoffs last year, averaging over 23 touches and 114 total yards from Weeks 15-18. He remains a volume-dependent RB2 option with little competition for carries.

Los Angeles

Key additions: RB Gus Edwards, LB Denzel Perryman, CB Kristian Fulton, TE Will Dissly, C Bradley Bozeman, DL Poona Ford, TE Hayden Hurst

Key losses: WR Mike Williams, WR Keenan Allen, WR Jaylen Guyton, RB Austin Ekeler, RB Joshua Kelley, TE Gerald Everett, C Will Clapp, LB Eric Kendricks, LB Kenneth Murray, CB Michael Davis

Key draft picks: OT Joe Alt, WR Ladd McConkey, LB Junior Colson, DT Justin Eboigbe, CB Tarheeb Still, CB Cam Hart, RB Kimani Vidal, WR Brenden Rice, WR Cornelius Johnson

The Chargers made headlines in the offseason by inking Jim Harbaugh to a five-year deal and experiencing a mass exodus of veterans - Austin Ekeler, Mike Williams, and Gerald Everett in free agency, and Keenan Allen in a trade to Chicago. To adapt Harbaugh's ultra-run-heavy scheme, the team selected tackle Joe Alt from Notre Dame and took a flier on Troy product Kimani Vidal in the sixth round. Vidal will split carries with veterans J.K. Dobbins and Gus Edwards, formerly of the Ravens. Justin Herbert greatly benefits from adding rookie Ladd McConkey from the University of Georgia, one of the best pure route-runners in the draft. He joins an unproven core of receivers, rounded out by Quentin Johnston and Joshua Palmer. Keeping Herbert upright within the pocket will go a long way toward speeding up the rebuilding effort in Los Angeles.

NFC East

Dallas

Key additions: LB Eric Kendricks, RB Ezekiel Elliott

Key losses: RB Tony Pollard, OT Tyron Smith, C Tyler Biadasz, DE Dorance Armstrong, De Dante Fowler Jr., DT Jonathan Hankins

Key draft picks: OT Tyler Guyton, EDGE Marshawn Kneeland, OG Cooper Beebe, LB Marist Liufau, CB Ryan Flournoy

Despite owner Jerry Jones's pledge to be "all in" during the offseason, the Cowboys have been quiet as a tomb since March, mainly due to salary cap constraints. Dallas desperately needs to sign Dak Prescott and CeeDee Lamb to long-term extensions after allowing several veterans (Tony Pollard, Tyron Smith, Tyler Biadasz) to leave in free agency. Rewarding Lamb for his outstanding 2023 campaign when he posted a career-high 135/1,749/12 split should take precedence. Dallas did their best to reinforce the offensive line through the draft, but banking on rookies to immediately gel and play at a high level is asking a great deal. The Cowboys lone skill position move occurred in early April when they brought back the corpse of Ezekiel Elliott, who has had one 1,000-yard rushing season since 2019. Elliott averaged a career-worst 3.5 YPC with the New England Patriots last year and will compete for touches with Rico Dowdle in the backfield. Head coach Mike McCarthy needs to make a deep playoff run to maintain job security, but all signs point to the team taking a step backward rather than forward.

New York

Key additions: DE Brian Burns, QB Drew Lock, RB Devin Singletary, WR Isaiah McKenzie, DB Jalen Mills, OL Jon Runyan Jr., OL Jermaine Eluemunor, TE Jack Stoll, OL Austin Schlottmann

Key losses: S Xavier McKinney, RB Saquon Barkley, QB Tyrod Taylor, DT A'Shawn Robinson

Key draft picks: WR Malik Nabers, S Tyler Nubin, CB Andru Phillips, TE Theo Johnson, RB Tyrone Tracy Jr.

Giants GM Joe Schoen heavily scouted rookie quarterbacks in the offseason, and many assumed the team would move on from Daniel Jones after another injury-riddled season. Unable to make a trade for North Carolina's Drake Maye, Schoen pivoted to selecting LSU receiver Malik Nabers instead, who has drawn comparisons to Ja'Marr Chase. His explosive ability and the presence of Jalin Hyatt, Darius Slayton, and Wan'Dale Robinson eliminate the "Jones doesn't have any weapons" excuse. New York heavily invested in the offensive line during free agency, bringing in several depth pieces, including Jermaine Eluemunor from Las Vegas, who can replace RT Evan Neal if he fails to improve. This is a "make or break" season for Jones after the Giants finished an embarrassing 31st in passing yards and 28th in passing touchdowns last year. New York lost Saquon Barkley in free agency to their arch-rival Philadelphia and signed Devin Singletary as his replacement. Already familiar with the offensive system due to his time in Buffalo, Singletary will search for his first 1,000-yard rushing season in 2024.

Philadelphia

Key additions: RB Saquon Barkley, OLB Bryce Huff, LB Devin White, S C.J. Gardner-Johnson, WR DeVante Parker, QB Kenny Pickett

Key losses: C Jason Kelce, OLB Haason Reddick, RB D'Andre Swift, DT Fletcher Cox, S Kevin Byard, QB Marcus Mariota

Key draft picks: CB Quinyon Mitchell, CB Cooper DeJean, EDGE Jalyx Hunt, RB Will Shipley, WR Ainias Smith, LB Jeremiah Trotter Jr., WR Johnny Wilson

After a blistering 10-1 start to the regular season, the Eagles fell apart, dropping five of their final six games before being crushed 32-9 by Tampa Bay in the wild-card round. In response, the team released its offensive and defensive coordinators, then heavily retooled during free agency and the draft. General manager Howie Roseman signed running back Saquon Barkley to a three-year deal before extending *DeVonta Smith and A.J. Brown to long-term extensions* to solidify the team's nucleus. Arguably one of the best one-two punches at wideout in the league, Smith and Brown are vying for their third-consecutive 1,000-yard season as a tandem. Meanwhile, Barkley will finally run behind an offensive line capable of opening up running lanes – a luxury he never received as a Giant. His massive upside makes him a mid-range RB1 for fantasy purposes. Philadelphia enters 2024 with high hopes to contend with San Francisco as the representative of the NFC in the Super Bowl – fingers crossed they don't fall like a house of cards under the weight of expectations again.

Washington

Key additions: C Tyler Biadasz, DE Dorance Armstrong, LB Bobby Wagner, LB Frankie Luvu, RB Austin Ekeler, QB Marcus Mariota, TE Zach Ertz, OG Nick Allegretti

Key losses: WR Curtis Samuel, CB Kendall Fuller, S Kamren Curl, QB Jacoby Brissett, QB Sam Howell, RB Antonio Gibson, LB Cody Barton

Key draft picks: QB Jayden Daniels, DT Jer'Zhan Newton, CB Mike Sainristil, TE Ben Sinnott, WR Luke McCaffrey, OG Brandon Coleman

The new ownership group in Washington is determined to eliminate the stigma of the Commanders being the doormat of the NFC East. With a common goal, they set to draft a new franchise quarterback in Heisman-winner Jayden Daniels from LSU, then surround him with an improved offensive line and upgraded backfield. Daniels brings a dual-threat capability to an offense that sorely lacked explosiveness in 2023, using his accuracy and mobility. Washington's offensive line surrendered the second-most sacks in the NFL last year at 65, a number that will need to improve for Daniels not to develop "happy feet" and become skittish. Veterans Zach Ertz, Austin Ekeler, and Terry McLaurin will provide outlets that Daniels can utilize at all field levels, with Jahan Dotson operating as the deep threat. Underappreciated in Fantasy circles, McLaurin will look to secure his fifth-straight season of over 77 receptions and 1,000 yards as the focal point in the passing attack. In the backfield, look for Ekeler to lead a committee situation as the main check-down option, with Brian Robinson being the short-yardage and goal-line back.

NFC North

Chicago

Key additions: WR Keenan Allen, RB D'Andre Swift, TE Gerald Everett, S Kevin Byard, C Ryan Bates

Key losses: QB Justin Fields, WR Darnell Mooney, RB D'Onta Freeman, DT Justin Jones

Key draft picks: QB Caleb Williams, WR Rome Odunze, OT Kiran Amegadije

It can be argued that no team in the NFL has improved as much since the conclusion of last season as Chicago. Generational talent Caleb Williams from USC is a perfect fit for offensive coordinator Shane Waldron's offense, which emphasizes pushing the ball downfield. Known for his improvisational talent and ability to pick apart defenses systematically, Williams is set up for instant success thanks to the exceptional trio of receivers at his disposal – D.J. Moore, Keenan Allen, and rookie Rome Odunze. Their presence compliments Williams's rushing upside – he surpassed double-digit touchdowns on the ground each of the last two seasons in college. Allen will function as a short-yardage outlet for Williams to target out of the slot, where he has been dominant for nearly a decade. Fantasy managers are crossing their collective fingers he remains healthy for the first time since 2021. Moore and Odunze are both elite downfield threats capable of outmuscling smaller defenders for contested catches, but their overlapping skill sets limit each other's point ceiling. D'Andre Swift experienced a career renaissance with Philadelphia last year, and Chicago will pair elusiveness with the bruising contrast of Roschon Johnson.

Detroit

Key additions: DT D.J. Reader, CB Carlton Davis, DE Marcus Davenport, CB Amik Robertson, OG Kevin Zeitler

Key losses: OG Jonah Jackson, CB Cameron Sutton, WR Josh Reynolds, S C.J. Gardner-Johnson, DT Benito Jones, QB Teddy Bridgewater

Key draft picks: CB Terrion Arnold, CB Ennis Rakestraw Jr., OT Giovanni Manu, S Sione Vaki

Tip of the cap to Detroit for hosting a phenomenal draft this year. Pegged as a breakout team before the year began, the Lions responded with a 12-5 record, clinching the NFC North for the first time since 1993 (when it was the NFC Central). Detroit's offense was stellar last year, finishing within the top 5 in passing yards, touchdown passes, rushing yards, and rushing touchdowns. Their well-balanced approach centered around the lethal play-action attack of Jared Goff and a magnificent one-two punch at running back. Finishing as the QB7 in fantasy last year, Goff has continued to fly under the radar as an underappreciated asset that can be drafted in the mid-rounds. David Montgomery and Jahmyr Gibbs finished with double-digit rushing touchdowns in 2023 and are the top thunder-and-lightning backfield committee in the league. When the Lions elect to pass the ball, one can expect it to land in the hands of either All-Pro Amon-Ra St.Brown (119/1,515/10 split in 2023) or standout tight end Sam LaPorta (86/889/10). Detroit is the only franchise operational for the entirety of the Super Bowl era that has not appeared in the big game. Expect that to change in short order.

Green Bay

Key additions: RB Josh Jacobs, S Xavier McKinney

Key losses: RB Aaron Jones, OG Jon Runyan, S Darnell Savage, LB De'Vondre Campbell, S Jonathan Owens

Key draft picks: OT Jordan Morgan, LN Edgerrin Cooper, S Javon Bullard, RB MarShawn Lloyd, LB Ty'Ron Hopper

A common question around the league last year was, "Can an incredibly young Packers team with no alpha wide receiver compete within a tough division?." Why yes, they can. Jordan Love proved that he has all the tools necessary to elevate the play of those around him, and he truly caught fire after Week 10, passing for two or more touchdowns in eight of his final nine games, with a 70.3% completion rate. His maturation was on full display during the Packers' dominating Wild Card win over Dallas, where he effectively picked apart their secondary. Green Bay seems intent on spreading the ball within their offense, not allowing defenders to hone in on one player. Last year, *seven* Packers had more than 40 targets, and only one had more than 60 receptions (Jayden Reed). For Fantasy, Reed can be valued slightly ahead of other Packer receivers, but the difference isn't drastic. The shift behind Love from Aaron Jones to Josh Jacobs is negligible. However, we are intrigued by the selection of rookie Marshawn Lloyd from Tennessee. His home-run hitting ability as a receiver and patience as a runner has us salivating in dynasty and keeper formats.

Minnesota

Key additions: OLB Jonathan Greenard, RB Aaron Jones, QB Sam Darnold, OLB Andrew Van Ginkel, LB Blake Cashman, DL Jonah Williams

Key losses: QB Kirk Cousins, OLB Danielle Hunter, OLB D.J. Wonnum, WR K.J. Osborn, OLB Marcus Davenport, RB Alexander Mattison, LB Jordan Hicks, QB Joshua Dobbs

Key draft picks: QB J.J. McCarthy, EDGE Dallas Turner, CB Khyree Jackson

Minnesota raised eyebrows shortly before the draft by acquiring the Houston Texans first-round pick, and all signs pointed towards the Vikings moving into the top five picks to develop a quarterback of their choice. Instead, Lady Luck smiled and said SKOL, dropping McCarthy right into their laps. McCarthy enters the most ready-for-success rookie landing spot in the league, surrounded by Justin Jefferson, Jordan Addison, and T.J. Hockenson. Expected to compete for the starting role right away, McCarthy will square off in a training camp battle opposite veteran Sam Darnold. At worst, it should only take a few weeks for McCarthy to start, and we would be patient with the situation. Reviewing McCarthy's collegiate tape at Michigan points out that he is a highly accurate passer off play-action (76% completion rate), but he also remains calm under pressure and is unphased by the blitz. Fantasy managers can expect Jefferson to continue to dominate targets as a locked-and-loaded WR1. Addison will see a slight bump in value early in the year when Hockenson continues to recover from the torn ACL/MCL he sustained last December. Hockenson is currently slated to miss the first month of the regular season.

NFC South

Atlanta

<u>Key additions:</u> QB Kick Cousins, WR Darnell Mooney, WR Rondale Moore, TE Charlie Woerner

<u>Key losses:</u> QB Desmond Ridder, RB Cordarrelle Patterson, TE Jonnu Smith, CB Jeff Okudah

<u>Key draft picks:</u> QB Michael Penix Jr., DT Ruke Orhorhoro, EDGE Bralen Trice, DT Brandon Dorlus

Atlanta caused quite a stir with their first-round selection of quarterback Michael Penix from Washington, less than two months after signing Kirk Cousins to a four-year, $180 million contract. At first glance, the decision seems odd, considering Penix's advanced age for a rookie and that, in a perfect situation, he would not see the field until the conclusion of Cousins' tenure – just in time for his rookie deal to almost expire. Switching our perspective to the "glass half full" view, at least the Falcons finally managed to ditch Arthur Smith and Desmond Ridder – a decision sure to spark their offense. All reports have Cousins expected to take the field in Week 1, fully recovered from his Achilles tear, but Penix will steal away valuable first-team reps until he is fully cleared to participate. Drake London and Kyle Pitts provide Cousins with a "can't miss" catch radius downfield, with Bijan Robinson and Rondale Moore running routes closer to the line of scrimmage. Newly hired offensive coordinator Zac Robinson will surely put the ball in the hands of Robinson more often than last season, and a primary breakout season is on the horizon.

Carolina

<u>Key additions:</u> WR Diontae Johnson, OG Robert Hunt, OG Damien Lewis, OLB Jadeveon Clowney, OLB D.J. Wonnum, DT A'Shawn Robinson, LB Josey Jewell, CB Dane Jackson, S Jordan Fuller, S Nick Scott

<u>Key losses:</u> OLB Brian Burns, LB Frankie Luvu, OLB Yetur Gross-Matos, CB C.J. Henderson, CB Donte Jackson, S Vonn Bell, S Jeremy Chinn, C Bradley Bozeman, TE Hayden Hurst

<u>Key draft picks:</u> WR Xavier Legette, RB Jonathon Brooks, LB Trevin Wallace, TE Ja'Tavion Sanders

It is easy to suggest that Carolina made the wrong decision in drafting Bryce Young over C.J. Stroud based on the early returns, but providing some context is a wise course of action. The Panthers' sieve offensive line allowed the second-most sacks in the league, forcing Young to scramble for his life constantly. Their poor performance also failed to allow plays to develop, resulting in a league-worst 5.5 YPA. Young's only trustworthy passing option was 33-year-old Adam Thielen, who had 60 more receptions than the next Panther player. So, is it honestly fair to judge a quarterback under constant duress with no legitimate threats? You be the judge. Thankfully, the team addressed several glaring holes through the NFL draft and spent three of their first four selections on bringing in offensive weapons for Young. Xavier Legette is a nightmare for opposing secondaries to cover due to his combination of size and speed, and he is set to assume the Chris Godwin role in Dave Canales' offense. Jonathon Brooks was ranked as the top running back within the class and should easily vault ahead of Chuba Hubbard and Miles Sanders in the Carolina depth chart. Fantasy managers must watch Brooks' availability to start the season since he suffered an ACL tear in November 2023.

New Orleans

<u>Key additions:</u> DE Chase Young, LB Willie Gay Jr., WR Cedrick Wilson Jr.

<u>Key losses:</u> QB Jameis Winston, DT Malcolm Roach, LB Zach Baun, CB Isaac Yiadom

<u>Key draft picks:</u> OT Taliese Fuaga, CB Kool-Aid McKinstry, QB Spencer Rattler, WR Bub Means

New Orleans's final 9-8 record was largely symbolic of their frustrating off-and-on season when they could not find consistency on either side of the ball. Derek Carr finished as the QB16 in fantasy, posting middle-of-the-road numbers in line with the rest of his career. The Saints' offense struggled out of the gate in 2023 due to Alvin Kamara's multi-game suspension, which pigeonholed what plays they could run. Even when on the field, it appeared that Kamara lost a step, as his 3.9 YPC was the second-lowest mark of his career, and he failed to record a rush over 17 yards. Instead, second-year receiver Chris Olave became New Orleans's go-to option, and he finished with universal career highs and an 87/1,123/5 split. Complemented by deep-threat Rashid Shaheed, the two players created a tandem that worked well to finish the season. First-round selection Taliese Fuaga will be charged with protecting Carr at right tackle and opening up holes in the run game, two areas in desperate need of improvement.

Tampa Bay

<u>Key additions:</u> S Jordan Whitehead, OG Sua Opeta, IOL Ben Bredeson, CB Tavierre Thomas

<u>Key losses:</u> OLB Shaquil Barrett, LB Devin White, CB Carlton Davis, OG Aaron Stinnie

<u>Key draft picks:</u> C Graham Barton, EDGE Chris Braswell, S Tykee Smith, WR Jalen McMillan, RB Bucky Irving

Tampa Bay was handsomely rewarded in their faith in Baker Mayfield, as he carried the team to a playoff berth in 2023 on the heels of a career year. Finishing as a top-10 option in passing yards (4.044) and touchdown passes (28), Mayfield was rewarded with a massive three-year, $115 M extension, and his presence will bring some stability to an aging roster. Rashaad White was the Buccaneers' lone option in the backfield last year, and an overwhelming volume (over 330 total touches) propelled him to an RB8 finish in Fantasy. White is a capable receiver and shifty in space, but his talents as a pure running back are middling at best. Tampa Bay's decision to select Bucky Irving will threaten White's upside and sap away several check-down opportunities. The dynamic duo of Mike Evans and Chris Godwin return as Mayfield's primary receiving weapons, with Godwin operating as the chain-moving threat and Evans the primary red-zone target. Evans will be on the hunt for his 11th consecutive 1,000-yard season, and his high-end, consistent production makes him a "set it and forget it" WR1 in fantasy.

NFC West

Arizona

<u>Key additions:</u> OT Jonah Williams, DT Justin Jones, DT Bilal Nichols, CB Sean Murphy-Bunting, WR Chris Moore, QB Desmond Ridder

<u>Key losses:</u> WR Marquise Brown, WR Rondale Moore, DT Leki Fotu

<u>Key draft picks:</u> WR Marvin Harrison Jr., EDGE Darius Robinson, CB Max Melton, RB Troy Benson, OT Isaiah Adams, TE Tip Reiman, CB Elijah Jones, S Dadrion Taylor-Demerson

Without Kyler Murray for half of the 2023 season, the Cardinals stumbled to a 4-13 finish and were the basement dwellers of the NFC West. Thankfully, the team wisely used their bevy of draft selections, bringing in a load of top-tier talent. Fourth-overall selection Marvin Harrison Jr. immediately becomes Arizona's top wideout, and expectations are sky-high for the most polished receiver to emerge from college in recent memory. The Cardinals also selected Florida State running back Trey Benson atop the third round – he demonstrated a unique blend of strength, acceleration, and patience in college and is a very adept receiver. Benson will siphon away some of James Conner's workload to start, with an outside chance of usurping him as the starter later in the season. Trey McBride finished as the TE7 in PPR scoring, thanks to a *massive* second-half breakout after veteran Zach Ertz went on IR with a quad injury. McBride will continue to have fantasy relevance as a mid-tier TE1 and the second option for Murray to target. Arizona should be much more competitive within the division if Murray remains healthy.

Los Angeles

<u>Key additions:</u> OG Jonah Jackson, CB Tre'Davious White, CB Darious Williams, S Kamren Curl, TE Colby Parkinson, QB Jimmy Garoppolo

<u>Key losses:</u> DT Aaron Donald, S Jordan Fuller, C Coleman Shelton, DL Jonah Williams, QB Carson Wentz

<u>Key draft picks:</u> EDGE Jared Verse, DT Braden Fiske, RB Blake Corum, S Kamren Kitchens, EDGE Brennan Jackson

Expected to have a down season in 2023, Los Angeles went so far as to send a letter to season ticket holders, warning them that it could be a long year. Instead, Los Angeles was one of the feel-good stories of 2023, on the heels of a record-setting campaign by rookie wideout Puka Nacua. Nacua set the new high mark for both receiving yards (1,486) and receptions (105) by a rookie and overtook Cooper Kupp as the alpha option for Matthew Stafford. With the band all back together again in 2024, fantasy managers should feel confident selecting Nacua as a WR1 and Kupp as a WR2, with Tyler Higbee and Kyren Williams being tertiary options. Fantasy managers should expect Williams to see a significant reduction in total touches following the decision to draft Michigan standout Blake Corum. Following the retirement news of All-Pro DT Aaron Donald, head coach Sean McVay was clear that there was no possible way to replace his presence directly. Instead, drafting multiple players along the defensive line with some of his attributes was the most feasible solution. For the Rams to stay within reach of the NFC West title, their top two defensive selections from Floria State must contribute immediately.

San Francisco

Key additions: DE Leonard Floyd, DE Yetur Gross-Matos, DT Maliek Collins, DT Jordan Elliott, LB De'Vondre Campbell, QB Joshua Dobbs

Key losses: DT Arik Armstead, DE Chase Young, QB Sam Darnold, De Clelin Ferrell, DT Javon Kinlaw, DT Sebastian Joseph, TE Charlie Woerner, DB Isaiah Oliver

Key draft picks: WR Ricky Pearsall, CB Renardo Green, OT Dominick Puni, S Malik Mustapha, RB Isaac Guerendo, WR Jacob Cowing

San Francisco's juggernaut team keeps rolling along and is hopeful that this will be the season they finally get to hoist the Lombardi trophy after unsuccessful attempts in 2013, 2020, and 2024. Simply put, this team has a few flaws, and they somehow became even better in the offseason. The 49ers selected Florida receiver Ricky Pearsall in the first round as insurance for Brandon Aiyuk and Deebo Samuel (both from a contract and injury standpoint). A former teammate of Aiyuk at Arizona State, Pearsall is an excellent route-runner who can dominate from Week 1 out of the slot. All-Pro options Christian McCaffrey and George Kittle return, giving Brock Purdy an embarrassment of riches to work around. McCaffrey, the consensus top selection in all of Fantasy, will look to repeat as the overall RB1. CMC's dominance can't be understated - he finished nearly 100 points ahead of the 2023 RB2, Raheem Mostert. Further upgrades along the line and secondary will strengthen an already imposing defense that led the league in interceptions (22) and finished as a top-10 unit in sacks and total yards allowed per game.

Seattle

Key additions: LB Jerome Baker, LB Tyrel Dodson, S Rayshawn Jenkins, DT Johnathan Hankins, CB K'Von Wallace, QB Sam Howell, OT George Fant

Key losses: LB Bobby Wagner, LB Jordyn Brooks, OG Damien Lewis, C Evan Brown, TE Colby Parkinson, TE Will Dissly, QB Drew Lock

Key draft picks: DT Byron Murphy, OG Christian Haynes, LB Tyrice Knight, TE AJ Barner

Seattle finished third in the NFC West last year due to struggles in the ground game – both getting their going and stopping the opposition's. The Seahawks finished an uncharacteristic fifth-worst in the league in total rushing yards, with the second-fewest rushing attempts. Ownership decided to move in a new direction by firing head coach Pete Carroll after 14 seasons and replacing him with former Baltimore Ravens defensive coordinator Mike Macdonald. Putting an immediate stamp on the team, Macdonald drafted the best interior defender in this year's draft, Byron Murphy II from Texas. Pairing him with Leonard Williams, Johnathan Hankins, and Dre'Mont Jones gives Seattle a formidable presence up front. Seattle hired Ryan Grubb from the University of Washington as their new offensive coordinator, who led one of the most prolific passing offenses in the country. Expect his presence to be a gigantic boon for DK Metcalf, Tyler Lockett, and Jaxon Smith-Nijgba (particularly Metcalf, who possesses similar alpha traits to former Huskies receiver Rome Odunze). Kenneth Walker led the Seahawks backfield with a 2:1 split over Zach Charbonnet and remains entrenched as a solid RB2 for fantasy.

Printed in Great Britain
by Amazon